中华古典文化精粹

THE ESSENCE OF CHINESE CLASSIC CULTORE

主　编:杨牧之
副主编:霍宝珍

Chief-Editor: Yang Muzhi
Deputy Chief-Editor: Huo Baozhen

老　子

Lao　zi

韦　利　英译
陈鼓应　今译
傅惠生　校注

Translated into Enylish by Waley
Translated into modern Chinese by Chen Guying
Revised and Annotated by Fu Huisheng

南海出版公司
Nanhai Publishing Company
2013 · 海口

前 言

这四种书我们选自驰名中外的汉英对照版《大中华文库》。《大中华文库》计划出版110种,目前已出版80余种。所选之书都是中华文明的精华,记载了中华民族五千年的历史和雄辉博大的民族精神。而这四种书更是其中的代表。

《论语》可以说是中国古代第一书。《论语》是“语言的论纂”,也就是“语录”的意思。它是孔子和他的弟子,以及弟子与弟子之间关于各种事物的讨论记录的汇编,是由孔子弟子及再传弟子编成的。《论语》内容涉及面很广,包括历史、政治、哲学、经济、艺术及道德伦理等方面内容,从中可以看出孔子对社会的理想,对政治的见解,对教育的主张,也可以看出孔子和他的弟子们的人格修养、治学态度和处世哲学。此书内容之广泛,影响之深远,堪称儒家经典。有人说:每个中国人一举手一投足所凸现出的中国气派,无不可从2400年前的一部经典《论语》中找到根源。可见,《论语》一书对中华民族传统文化的形成起了重大的作用。

《道德经》* 五千言,凝聚了中华民族的智慧,体现了中国古代的先贤对宇宙的看法,对人生的总结。它是中国哲学史上第一部具有完整哲学体系的著作。仅凭这一点《道德经》在中国历史上就具有举足轻重的地位。《道德经》的作者是老子,是道家思想的奠基者。他的真名叫李耳,当时人多称其为老聃。据说孔子曾向他请教过有关“礼”的知识,所

* 《道德经》,又叫《老子》。——编者注

以，可以说是孔子的老师。“道”和“德”是老子哲学思想的理论基础。老子的“道”有丰富的含义，他认为“道”先天地而存在，是万物的本原，天地万物都从“道”中产生。“德”则是“道”的显现和展开。老子关注的都是天下、国家、社会的大事，他的哲学思想，借助天道，关照人道，指导治国和修身，主张“无为而治”，“贵柔”，顺应自然，韬晦自保，建立了有鲜明个性的道家体系。著名的话是：“我无为，而民自化；我好静，而民自正；我无事，而民自富；我无欲，而民自朴。”还说：“天下莫柔弱于水，而攻坚强者莫之能胜。”“不敢为天下先。”这些精彩的言论，很令人深思。西方的学者说：从来没有一本书内容如此丰富而篇幅又如此短小，真可谓博大精深。

《孙子兵法》早已享誉世界，被誉为“兵经”，作者孙武被誉为“兵圣”。英国的军事家蒙哥马利元帅说：世界上所有的军事学院都应把《孙子兵法》列为必修课。如今，人们不但用《孙子兵法》指导战争，还用他指导企业发展。日本学者村上孚说：日本企业的生存发展有两大支柱，一是美国的现代管理制度，一是《孙子兵法》的战略和策略。据统计，它已有 29 种文字的译本在世界流传。在全世界产生了广泛而深刻的影响。说到《孙膑兵法》更是十分有趣。因为《孙膑兵法》早已失传，人们见不到原书，所以千百年来争论不休。到底有没有孙膑其人，有没有孙膑其书，众说纷纭。直到 1972 年，山东临沂银雀山汉墓同时出土了《孙子兵法》和《孙膑兵法》，争论顿消。孙膑是孙武的后代子孙，曾和庞涓一起学习兵法。庞涓忌妒孙膑的才华，把孙膑骗到魏国，“断其两足而黥之”。《史记·太史公自序》说：“孙子膑脚而论兵法。”就是说的孙膑被庞涓害了之后，发愤著书。孙膑的“围魏救赵”，功其必救的战法，已成为中外军事史上避实就虚的著名战例。“增兵减灶”，制造假象诱敌就范的战法，也成为历史上著名的战例。《孙膑兵法》继承了《孙子兵法》的体系和风格，是《孙子兵法》之后又一部影响深远的军事著作。

这四部著作，言简意赅。《论语》约16000字，《道德经》约5400字，《孙子兵法》十三篇约6000多字，《孙膑兵法》11000字。总计不足40000字。但是围绕它们所产生的研究著作岂止成千上万。如今它们已成为世界文化瑰宝，读者遍天下。所以，这几部书是不能不读的。这也就是为什么我们选这四部书介绍给大家的原因。

本书的体例，每本书都由三部分组成，先是中国古文原文，然后是古文译成的中国白话文，最后是译成的英文。这样就既方便学汉语的人阅读，也方便学英语的人阅读。

我们力图做得精致，但由于时间仓促，还有许多不如意处，容日后再版时改正。

杨俊

2013年3月

INTRODUCTION

The four books are selected from the world known Chinese-English Library of Chinese Classics, in which more than 80 kinds of book have been published among 110 kinds of books which are planned to publish. The Library of Chinese Classics, as the essence of Chinese civilization, records Chinese 5,000-years history and demonstrate the national spirit of China. Four of these books, selected in our series, stand out: *The Analects*, *Dao De Jing*, *Sunzi*: *The Art of War and Sun Bin*: *The Art of War*, which are extremely reflected within them.

The Analects, also know as the collection of Confucius' talks, are mostly described as an ancient book with the heaviest influence on Chinese culture. It records discussions on various opinions of the world between Confucius and his students and among his students which were later complied into a book by his students and their successors. It covers a wide ranges history, politics, philosophy, economy, art and moral ethnics. It demonstrates Confucius' idea towards society, politics and education, and also reflects the moral quality, the meticulous scholarship and living philosophy of Confucius and his students. Due to the wide coverage and far-reaching impacts of this book, it can be regarded as real confucianism classics. Someone observe that the "Chineseness" expressed by every Chinese in his daily behaviors are all originated from the classical "The Analects", a cla ssic piece 2400 years ago. It is obvious that *The Analects* has played important roles in forming the Chinese traditional civilization.

Dao De Jing * ,condenses the collective wisdom of the Chinese nation, represents the idea towards universe and summary towards life of our past scholars. It is the first systematically philosophical work in Chinese history of philosophy, even only by this can grant it prove decisive position in China's history. The writer of *Dao De Jing*, Laozi, is the forerunner of Taoist school of Chinese philosophy. His real name is Li Er, and was addressed as Lao Dan. It is said that Confucius used to consult him on the issue of *Li*(礼), thus to some extent he was the teacher of Confucius. The essence of his philosophical core is *Dao*(道) and *De*(德). According to Laozi, *Dao* (道) existed before Nature; *Dao* (道) is the basic category of the universe; everything in Nature generated from *Dao*(道). *De* (德) is the revelation and expansion of *Dao* (道). What Laozi was concerned was the great matters of the universe, the nation and the community. His philosophical thoughts are about the law of Nature, humanity, country governance and morality cultivation. "Regulatethrough actionless activity", "emphasis on softness", conforming to Nature, hiding talents and self preservation are the concepts of his distinctive Taoism ideal. His famous saying includes:

"So long as I do nothing, the people will of themselves be transformed. So long as I love quietude, the people will of themselves go straight. So long as I act only by inactivity the people

---

* Editors' Note: *Dao De Jing*, also know as *Laozi*.

will of themselves become prosperous. So long as I have no wants the people will of themselves return to the ' state of the Uncarved Block'. "

"Nothing under heaven is softer or more yielding than water. "

"Refusal to be foremost of all things under heaven. "

All these amazing analects of Laozi are provokative for us. Western scholars comment that there is no book that has such rich connotation and is as concise as Moral Classics. The profound wisdom contained in the book is incomparable.

Sunzi: *The Art of War* has long been held in high esteem worldwide as the "military classic" and its author *Sunzi*, whose full name is Sun Wu has been revered as "military genius". The England militarist Bernard Law Montgomery used to suggest opening a compulsory course in every military institutes on *Sunzi*: *The Art of War*. Nowadays it is applied as the guidance not only of wars but also of the development of enterprises. In accordance Murakami Makoto, a Japanese scholar, along with American management system, the strategies embedded in *Sunzi*: *The Art of War* has become the other pillar to sustain the development of Japanese enterprises. It is estimated that it has been translated into 29 different languages. It has brought fundamental impacts on the whole world.

There is an interesting story about *Su Bin*: *The Art of War*. Since the original book had disappeared for a long time, people argued the existence of this book and even Sun Bin for hundreds of years. Until 1972, two sets of bamboo strips, *Sunzi*: *The Art of War* and *Sun Bin*: *The Art of War* were unearthed in a cemetery of Han Dynasty at Yin Que Shan (Silver Sparrow Mountain) in Linyi Country, Shan Dong province that all the arguments faded away. Sun Bin was a descendent of Sun Wu by several generations, the author of *Sunzi: The Art of War*. He once studied with Pang Juan, who became jealous of Sun Bin's talent and deceived him to Wei (魏) State, where Sun Bin was cut his legs but continued to devote himself in the art of war. This story could be located in the *Autobiographic Notes of Tai Shi Gong* (太史公自序, *Tai Shi Gong Zixu*). Some famous strategies created by Sun Bin, such as "besiege Wei to rescue Zhao", which has become the famous case of evading the enemy's main force and striking his weak points in the military history at home and abroad. In addition, "increasing the troop while decreasing the stoves" so as to induce and trap the opponent also sets a typical example of warfare throughout the history. *Sun Bin: The Art of War* inherited the same system and style of its predecessor. And *Sunzi: The Art of War*, becomes another influential works in Chinese military history.

These four works are concise and comprehensive—in total the length of these four works does not go beyond 40,000 words, among which about 16,000 for *The Analects*, 5,4000 for *Dao De Jing*, 6,000 for *Sunzi: The Art of War*, and 11,000 for *Sun Bin: The Art of War*. But there are thousands of works to study them. Given their world-wide influence and significance and wide readership, they have become the gems of global culture. That is the reason we picked up these four works to publish.

This book consists of three parts: the first part is the original version written by classic Chinese; the second part is the translated version in vernacular Chinese; and then comes the English version. Hence this series of book is open to both Chinese-learner and English-learners.

We tried to design and typeset this series of works perfectly, but given the limited time there is still some room for improvement. Thus any comment is appreciated.

Yang Muzhi

Translated by Li Qiushuang

Mar. 2013

目　录

CONTENTS

第一章

【原文】

道可道,非常“道”;名可名,非常“名”。

“无”,名天地之始;“有”,名万物之母。

故常“无”,欲以观其妙;

常“有”,欲以观其徼。

此两者,同出而异名,同谓之玄。

玄之又玄,众妙之门。

【今译】

可以用言词表达的道,就不是常“道”;可以说得出来的名,就不是常“名”。

“无”,是天地的本始;“有”,是万物的根源。

所以常从“无”中,去观照“道”的奥妙;常从“有”中,去观照“道”的端倪。

“无”和“有”这两者,同一来源而不同名称,都可说是深远莫测的,从有形的深远境界到达无形的深远境界,这就是一切变化的总门径。

Chapter 1

The Way that can be told of is not an Unvarying Way;

The names that can be named are not unvarying names.

It was from the Nameless that Heaven and Earth sprang;

The named is but the mother that rears the ten thousand creatures, each after its kind. [1]

Truly, "Only he that rids himself forever of desire can see the Secret Essences";

He that has never rid himself of desire can see only the Outcomes. [2]

These two things issued from the same mould, but nevertheless are different in name.

This "same mould" we can but call the Mystery,

Or rather the "Darker than any Mystery", [3]

The Doorway whence issued all Secret Essences. [4]

第二章

【原文】

天下皆知美之为美，斯恶已；皆知善之为善，斯不善已。

有无相生，难易相成，长短相形，高下相盈，音声相和，前后相随，恒也。

是以圣人处无为之事，行不言之教；万物作而弗始，生而弗有，为而弗恃，功成而弗居。夫唯弗居，是以不去。

【今译】

天下都知道美之所以为美，丑的观念也就产生了；都知道善之所以为善，不善的观念也就产生了。

有和无互相生成，难和易互相完成，长和短互相形成，高和下互相包含，音和声互相和调，前和后在对立中互相区分，这是永远如此的。

所以有道的人以“无为”的态度来处理世事，实行“不言”的教导；让万物兴起而不加倡导；生养万物而不据为己有；作育万物而不自恃己能；功业成就而不自我夸耀。正因他不自我夸耀，所以他的功绩不会泯没。

Chapter 2

It is because every one under Heaven recognizes beauty as beauty, that the idea of ugliness exists. [1]

And equally if every one recognized virtue[2] as virtue, this would merely create fresh conceptions of wickedness.

For truly, Being and Not-being grow out of one another;

Difficult and easy complete one another.

Long and short test one another;

High and low determine one another.

Pitch and mode give harmony to one another.

Front and back give sequence to one another.

Therefore[3] the Sage relies on actionless activity[4],

Carries on wordless teaching,

But the myriad creatures are worked upon by him; he does not disown them[5].

He rears them, but does not lay claim to them,

Controls them, but does not lean upon them.

Achieves his aim, but does not call attention to what he does;

And for the very reason that he does not call attention to what he does.

He is not ejected from fruition of what he has done.

第三章

【原文】

不尚贤,使民不争;不贵难得之货,使民不盗;不见可欲,使民心不乱。

是以圣人之治,虚其心,实其腹,弱其志,强其骨。常使民无知无欲。使夫智者不敢为也。为无为,则无不治。

【今译】

不标榜贤才异能,使人民不争功名;不珍贵难得的财货,使人民不做盗贼;不显耀可贪的事物,使人民不被惑乱。

所以有道的人治理政事,要净化人民的心思,满足人民的安饱,减损人民的心志,增强人民的体魄。常使人民没有(伪诈的)心智,没有(争盗的)欲念。使一些自作聪明的人不敢妄为。以"无为"的态度去处理事务,就没有不上轨道的。

Chapter 3

If we stop looking for "persons of superior morality" (hien)[1] to put in power, there will be no more jealousies among the people. If we cease to set store by products that are hard to get, there will be no more thieves. If the people never see such things as excite desire, their hearts will remain placid and undisturbed. Therefore the Sage rules:

By emptying their hearts[2]
And filling their bellies,
Weakening their intelligence
And toughening their sinews,
Ever striving to make the people knowledgeless and desireless.

Indeed he sees to it that if there be any who have knowledge, they dare not interfere.

Yet through his actionless activity all things are duly regulated.

第四章

【原文】

道冲,而用之或不盈。
渊兮,似万物之宗;
(挫其锐,解其纷;
和其光,同其尘;)
湛兮,似或存。
吾不知谁之子,象帝之先。

【今译】

“道”体是虚空的,
然而作用却不穷竭。
渊深啊! 它好像是万物的主宰;
(不露锋芒,消解纷扰;
含敛光耀,混同尘世;)
幽隐啊! 似亡而又实存。
我不知道它是从哪里产生的,
似乎在有天地以前就有了它。

Chapter 4

The Way is like an empty vessel
That yet may be drawn from
Without ever needing to be filled.

It is bottomless; the very progenitor of all things in the world[1].

(In it all sharpness is blunted,
All tangles untied,
All glare tempered,
All dust soothed.)[2]

It is like a deep pool that never dries.[3]

Was it too the child of something else? We cannot tell.

But as a substanceless image it existed before the Ancestor.[4]

第五章

【原文】

天地不仁，以万物为刍狗；圣人不仁，以百姓为刍狗。

天地之间，其犹橐籥乎！虚而不屈，动而愈出。

多言数穷，不如守中。

【今译】

天地无所偏爱，任凭万物自然生长；“圣人”无所偏爱，任凭百姓自己发展。

天地之间，岂不像个风箱吗？空虚但不会穷竭，发动起来而生生不息。

议论太多，反而加速败亡，不如持守虚静。

Chapter 5

Heaven and Earth are ruthless;[1]
To them the Ten Thousand Things are but as straw dogs.[2]
The Sage too is ruthless;[3]
To him the people are but as straw dogs.
Yet Heaven and Earth and all that lies between
Is like a bellows
In that it is empty, but gives a supply that never fails.
Work it, and more comes out.
Whereas the force of words is soon spent.
Far better is it to keep what is in the heart.[4]

第六章

【原文】

谷神不死，是谓玄牝。
玄牝之门，是谓天地根。
绵绵若存，用之不勤。

【今译】

虚空的变化是永不停竭的，这就是微妙的母性。
微妙的母性之门，是天地的根源。
它连绵不绝地永存着，愈用愈出，无穷无尽。

Chapter 6

The Valley Spirit never dies.[1]
It is named the Mysterious Female.[2]
And the Doorway of the Mysterious Female
Is the base from which Heaven and Earth sprang.
It is there within us all the while;
Draw upon it as you will, it never runs dry.[3]

第七章

【原文】

天长地久。天地所以能长且久者,以其不自生,故能长生。

是以圣人后其身而身先;外其身而身存。非以其无私邪?故能成其私。

【今译】

天地是长久存在的。天地所以能够长久,乃是因为它们的一切运作都不是为了自己,所以能够长久。

所以有道的人把自己放在后面,反而能赢得爱戴;把自己生命置于度外,反而能保全生命。不正是由于他不自私吗?反而能达到自私的目的。

Chapter 7

Heaven is eternal, the Earth everlasting.

How come they to be so? It is because they do not foster their own lives;[1]

That is why they live so long.[2]

Therefore the Sage

Puts himself in the background; but is always to the fore.

Remains outside; but is always there.[3]

It is not just because he does not strive for any personal end

That all his personal ends are fulfilled?[4]

第八章

【原文】

上善若水。水善利万物而不争，处众人之所恶，故几于“道”。

居善地，心善渊，与善仁，言善信，政善治，事善能，动善时。

夫唯不争，故无尤。

【今译】

最善的人好像水一样。水善于滋润万物而不和万物相争，停留在大家所不愿处的地方，所以最接近于“道”。

居处善于选择地方，心胸善于保持沉静，待人善于真诚相爱，说话善于遵守信用，为政善于精简处理，处事善于发挥所长，行动善于掌握时机。

只因为有不争的美德，所以没有过错。

老子

Chapter 8

The highest good is like that of water. [1] The goodness of water is that it benefits the ten thousand creatures; yet itself does not scramble, but is content with the places that all men disdain. It is this that makes water so near to the Way.

And if men think the ground the best place for building a house upon,

If among thoughts they value those that are profound,

If in friendship they value gentleness,

In words, truth; in government, good order;

In deeds, effectiveness; in actions, timeliness—[2]

In each case it is because they prefer what does not lead to strife,

And therefore does not go amiss.

第九章

【原文】

持而盈之,不如其已;
揣而锐之,不可长保。
金玉满堂,莫之能守;
富贵而骄,自遗其咎。
功遂身退,天之道也。

【今译】

执持盈满,不如适时停止;
显露锋芒,锐势难保长久。
金玉满堂,无法守藏;
富贵而骄,自取祸患。
功业完成,含藏收敛,
是合于自然的道理。

Chapter 9

Stretch a bow[1] to the very full,
And you will wish you had stopped in time;
Temper a sword-edge to its very sharpest,
And you will find it soon grows dull.
When bronze[2] and jade fill your hall.
It can no longer be guarded.
Wealth and place breed insolence
That brings ruin in its train.
When your work is done, then withdraw![3]
Such is Heaven's Way.[4]

第十章

【原文】

载营魄抱一,能无离乎?
专气致柔,能婴儿乎?
涤除玄览,能无疵乎?
爱民治国,能无为乎?
天门开阖,能为雌乎?
明白四达,能无知乎?
(生之畜之。生而不有,为而不恃,
长而不宰,是谓"玄德"。)

【今译】

精神和形体合一,能不分离吗?
结聚精气以致柔顺,能像无欲的婴儿吗?
洗清杂念而深入观照,能没有瑕疵吗?
爱民治国,能自然无为吗?
感官和外界接触,能守静吗?
通晓四方,能不用心机吗?

(生长万物,养育万物。生长而不占有,畜养而不依恃,导引而不主宰,这就是最深的"德"。)

Chapter 10

Can you keep the unquiet physical-soul[1] from straying, hold fast to the Unity, and never quit it?

Can you, when concentrating your breath, make it soft like that of a little child?

Can you wipe and cleanse your vision of the Mystery[2] till all is without blur?

Can you love the people and rule the land, yet remain unknown?[3]

Can you in opening and shutting the heavenly gates play always the female part?

Can your mind penetrate every corner of the land, but you yourself never interfere?

(Rear them, then, feed them,
Rear them, but do not lay claim to them.
Control them, but never lean upon them;
Be chief among them, but do not manage them.
This is called the Mysterious Power.)[4]

第十一章

【原文】

三十辐共一毂，
当其无，有车之用。
埏埴以为器，
当其无，有器之用。
凿户牖，以为室，
当其无，有室之用。
故有之以为利，
无之以为用。

【今译】

三十根辐条汇集到一个毂当中，车毂中有了空的地方，才有车的作用。

糅合陶土做成器具，器皿中有了空的地方，才有器皿的作用。

开凿门窗建造房屋，门窗四壁中有了空的地方，才有房屋的作用。

所以“有”给人便利，须靠“无”发挥作用。

Chapter 11

We put thirty spokes together and call it a wheel;[1]

But it is on the space where there is nothing that the usefulness of the wheel depends.

We turn clay to make a vessel;

But it is on the space where there is nothing that the usefulness of the vessel depends.

We pierce doors and windows to make a house;

And it is on these spaces where there is nothing that the usefulness of the house depends.

Therefore just as we take advantage of what is, we should recognize the usefulness of what is not.[2]

第十二章

【原文】

五色令人目盲；
五音令人耳聋；
五味令人口爽；
驰骋畋猎，令人心发狂；
难得之货，令人行妨。
是以圣人为腹不为目，
故去彼取此。

【今译】

缤纷的色彩使人眼花缭乱；
纷杂的音调使人听觉不敏；
饮食餍饫会使人舌不知味；
纵情狩猎使人心放荡；
稀有物品使人行为不轨；

因此圣人但求安饱而不逐声色之娱，所以摒弃物欲的诱惑而保持安足的生活。

Chapter 12

The five colours confuse the eye,
The five sounds dull the ear,
The five tastes spoil the palate.
Excess of hunting and chasing
Makes minds go mad. [1]
Products that are hard to get
Impede their owner's movements.
Therefore the Sage
Considers the belly not the eye,
Truly, "he rejects that but takes this." [2]

第十三章

【原文】

宠辱若惊,贵大患若身。

何谓宠辱若惊?宠为下,得之若惊,失之若惊,是谓宠辱若惊。

何谓贵大患若身?吾所以有大患者,为吾有身,及吾无身,吾有何患?

故贵以身为天下,若于寄天下;爱以身为天下,若可托天下。

【今译】

得宠和受辱都使人感到惊慌失措,重视身体好像重视大患一样。

什么叫作得宠和受辱感到惊慌失措?得宠仍是下等的,得到恩惠感到心惊不安,失去恩惠也觉惊恐慌乱,这就叫作得宠和受辱感到惊慌失措。

什么叫作重视身体像重视大患一样?我所以有大患,乃是因为我有这个身体,如果没有这个身体,我会有什么大患呢?

所以能够以贵身的态度去为天下,才可以把天下寄托给他;以爱身的态度去爱天下,才可以把天下委托给他。

Chapter 13

"Favour and disgrace goad as it were to madness; high rank hurts keenly as our bodies hurt."[1]

What does it mean to say that favour and disgrace goad as it were to madness? It means that when a ruler's subjects get it they turn distraught,[2] when they lose it they turn distraught. That is what is meant by saying favour and disgrace goad as it were to madness. What does it mean to say that high rank hurts keenly as our bodies hurt? The only reason that we suffer hurt is that we have bodies; if we had no bodies, how could we suffer?

Therefore we may accept the saying: "He who in dealing with the empire regards his high rank as though it were his body[3] is the best person to be entrusted with rule; he who in dealing with the empire loves his subjects as one should love one's body is the best person to whom one can commit the empire."

第十四章

【原文】

视之不见，名曰“夷”；听之不闻，名曰“希”；搏之不得，名曰“微”。此三者不可致诘，故混而为一。

其上不皦，其下不昧。绳绳兮不可名，复归于无物。是谓无状之状，无物之象，是谓惚恍。迎之不见其首；随之不见其后。

执古之道，以御今之有。能知古始，是谓道纪。

【今译】

看它看不见，名叫“夷”；听它听不到，名叫“希”；摸它摸不着，名叫“微”。这三者的形象无从推问，它是浑然一体的。

它上面不显得光亮，它下面也不显得阴暗，它绵绵不绝而不可名状，一切的运动都会还回到不见物体的状态。这是没有形状的形状，不见物体的形象，叫它作“惚恍”。迎着它，看不见它的前头；随着它却看不见它的后面。

把握着早已存在的“道”，来驾驭现在的具体事物。能够了解宇宙的原始，叫作“道”的规律。

Chapter 14

Because the eye gazes but can catch no glimpse of it,
It is called elusive.
Because the ear listens but cannot hear it,
It is called the rarefied.
Because the hand feels for it but cannot find it,
It is called the infinitesimal.
These three, because they cannot be further scrutinized,
Blend into one.
Its rising brings no light;
Its sinking, no darkness.[1]
Endless the series of things without name
On the way back to where there is nothing.
They are called shapeless shapes;
Forms without form;
Are called vague semblances.
Go towards them, and you can see no front;
Go after them, and you see no rear.
Yet by seizing on the Way that was
You can ride[2] the things that are now.
For to know what once there was,[3] in the Beginning,
This is called the essence[4] of the Way.[5]

第十五章

【原文】

古之善为道者,微妙玄通,深不可识。夫唯不可识,故强为之容:

豫兮其若冬涉川;犹兮其若畏四邻;

俨兮其若客;涣兮其若凌释;

敦兮其若朴;旷兮其若谷;

混兮其若浊;

(澹兮其若海;飂兮若无止。)

孰能浊以静之徐清;孰能安以动之徐生。

保此道者不欲盈。夫唯不盈,故能敝而新成。

【今译】

古时善于行道的人,精妙通达,深刻而难以认识。正因为难以认识,所以勉强对他进行描绘:

小心审慎啊,像冬天涉足江河;

警觉戒惕啊,像提防四周的围攻;

拘谨严肃啊,像作宾客;

融和可亲啊,像冰柱消融;

淳厚朴质啊,像未经雕琢的素材;

空豁开广啊,像深山的幽谷;

浑朴淳厚啊,像浊水的样子;

(沉静恬淡啊,好像湛深的大海;

飘逸无系啊,好像无有止境。)

谁能在动荡中安静下来而慢慢地澄清?

谁能在安定中变动起来而慢慢地趋进？

保持这些道理的人不肯自满。只因为他不自满，所以能去故更新。

Chapter 15

Of old those that were the best officers of Court[1]

Had inner natures subtle, abstruse, mysterious, penetrating,

Too deep to be understood.

And because such men could not be understood

I can but tell of them as they appeared to the world:

Circumspect they seemed, like one who in winter crosses a stream;

Watchful, as one who must meet danger on every side.

Ceremonious, as one who pays a visit;

Yet yielding, as ice when it begins to melt.

Blank, as a piece of uncarved wood;

Yet receptive as a hollow in the hills.

Murky, as a troubled stream—

(Tranquil, as the vast reaches of the sea,

Drifting, as the wind with no stop.)[2]

Which of you can assume such murkiness, to become in the end still and clear?

Which of you can make yourself inert, to become in the end full of life and stir?

Those who possess this Tao do not try to fill themselves to the brim,

And because they do not try to fill themselves to the brim,

They are like a garment that endures all wear and need never be renewed.[3]

第十六章

【原文】

致虚极，守静笃。
万物并作，吾以观其复。
夫物芸芸，各复归其根。
归根曰静，静曰复命。
复命曰常，知常曰明。
不知常，妄作凶。
知常容，容乃公，
公乃全，全乃天，
天乃道，道乃久，
没身不殆。

【今译】

致虚和守静的功夫，做到极笃的境地。

万物蓬勃生长，我看出往复循环的道理。

万物纷纷纭纭，各自返回到它的本根。返回本根叫作静，静叫作复命。复命叫作常，了解常叫作明。不了解常，轻举妄动就会出现乱子。

了解常道的人是无所不包的，无所不包就能坦然大公，坦然大公才能无不周遍，无不周遍才能符合自然，符合自然才能符合于道，体道而行才能长久，终身可免于危殆。

Chapter 16

Push far enough towards the Void,
Hold fast enough to Quietness,
And of the ten thousand things none but can be worked on by you.
I have beheld them, whither they go back.
See, all things howsoever they flourish
Return to the root from which they grew.
This return to the root is called Quietness;
Quietness is called submission to Fate;
What has submitted to Fate has become part of the always-so.
To know the always-so is to be illumined;
Not to know it, means to go blindly to disaster.
He who knows the always-so has room in him for everything;
He who has room in him for everything is without prejudice.
To be without prejudice is to be kingly;[1]
To be kingly is to be of heaven;[2]
To be of heaven is to be in Tao.
Tao is forever and he that possesses it,
Though his body ceases, is not destroyed.[3]

第十七章

【原文】

太上,不知有之;
其次,亲而誉之;
其次,畏之;
其次,侮之。
信不足焉,有不信焉。
悠兮其贵言。
功成事遂,
百姓皆谓:“我自然。”

【今译】

最好的世代,人民根本感觉不到统治者的存在;其次,人民亲近而赞美他;再其次的,人民畏惧他;更其次的,人民轻侮他。

统治者的诚信不足,人民自然不相信他。

(最好的统治者)却是悠然而不轻于发号施令。事情办成功了,百姓都说:“我们本来是这样的。”

Chapter 17

Of the highest the people merely know[1] that such a one exists;

The next they draw near to and praise.

The next they shrink from, intimated; but revile.

Truly, "It is by not believing people that you turn them into liars."[2]

But from the Sage it is so hard at any price to get a single word

That when his task is accomplished, his work done,

Throughout the country everyone says, "It happened of its own accord."

第十八章

【原文】

大道废，有仁义；
智慧出，有大伪；
六亲不和，有孝慈；
国家昏乱，有忠臣。

【今译】

大道废弃，才提倡仁义；
智巧出现，才产生伪诈；
家庭纠纷，才显出孝慈；
国家昏乱，才见出忠臣。

Chapter 18

It was when the Great Way declined
That human kindness and morality[1] arose;
It was when intelligence and knowledge appeared
That the Great Artifice began.
It was when the six near ones[2] were no longer at peace
That there was talk of "dutiful sons"; [3]
Nor till fatherland was dark with strife
Did we hear of "loyal slaves."[4]

第十九章

【原文】

绝圣弃智,民利百倍;
绝仁弃义,民复孝慈;
绝巧弃利,盗贼无有。
此三者以为文不足。
故令有所属:
见素抱朴,少私寡欲,绝学无忧。

【今译】

抛弃聪明和智巧,人民可以得到百倍的好处;
抛弃仁和义,人民可以恢复孝慈的天性;
抛弃巧诈和私利,盗贼就自然会消失。
(圣智、仁义、巧利)这三者全是巧饰的,
不足以治理天下。

所以要使人有所归属:保持淳朴,减少私欲,抛弃(圣智礼法的)学问,没有忧虑。

Chapter 19

Banish wisdom, discard knowledge,
And the people will be benefited a hundredfold.
Banish human kindness, discard morality,
And the people will be dutiful and compassionate.
Banish skill, discard profit,
And thieves and robbers will disappear.
If when these three things are done they find life too plain and unadorned,
Then let them have accessories;
Give them Simplicity to look at,
The Uncarved Block to hold,
Give them selflessness and fewness of desires.
Banish learning, and there will be no more grieving. [1]

第二十章

【原文】

唯之与阿，相去几何？美之与恶，相去若何？人之所畏，不可不畏。

荒兮，其未央哉！

众人熙熙，如享太牢，如春登台。

我独泊兮，其未兆；沌沌兮，如婴儿之未孩；累累兮，若无所归。

众人皆有余，而我独若遗。

我愚人之心也哉！

俗人昭昭，我独昏昏。俗人察察，我独闷闷。

（澹兮其若海，飂兮若无止。）

众人皆有以，而我独顽且鄙。我独异于人，而贵食母。

【今译】

应诺和呵声，相差好多？所谓美好和丑恶相差好多？人们所畏惧的，也不必去触犯。

精神领域开阔啊，好像没有尽头的样子！

众人兴高采烈，好像参加丰盛的筵席，又像春天登台眺望景色。

而我独个儿淡泊宁静啊，不炫耀自己；混混沌沌啊，好像不知嬉笑的婴儿；闲闲散散啊，好像无家可归。

众人都有多余，惟独我好像不足的样子。

我真是“愚人”的心肠啊！

世人都光耀自炫，惟独我昏昏昧昧的样子。

世人都精明灵巧，惟独我无所识别的样子。

沉静恬淡啊，好像湛深的大海，飘逸无奈啊，好像没有止境。

众人都好像很有作为，惟独我愚昧而笨拙。

我和世人不同，而重视进“道”的生活。

Chapter 20

Between wei and o[1]
What after all is the difference?
Can it be compared to the difference between good and bad?
The saying "what others avoid I too must avoid"
How false and superficial it is![2]
All men, indeed, are wreathed in smiles,
As though feasting after the Great Sacrifice,
As though going up to the Spring Carnival.
I alone am inert, like a child that has not yet given sign;
Like an infant that has not yet smile.
I droop and drift, as though I belonged nowhere.
All men have enough and to spare;
I alone seem to have lost everything.[3]
Mine is indeed the mind of a very idiot,
So dull am I.
The world is full of people that shine;
I alone am dark.
They look lively and self-assured;
I alone depressed.
(I seem unsettled as the ocean;
Blown adrift, never brought to a stop.)[4]
All men can be put to some use;
I alone am intractable and boorish.
But wherein I most am different from men
Is that I prize no sustenance that comes not from the Mother's[5] breast.

第二十一章

【原文】

孔“德”之容,惟“道”是从。
“道”之为物,惟恍惟惚。
惚兮恍兮,其中有象;
恍兮惚兮,其中有物。
窈兮冥兮,其中有精。
其精甚真,其中有信。
自今及古,其名不去,
以阅众甫。
吾何以知众甫之状哉!
以此。

【今译】

大“德”的样态,随着“道”而转移。

“道”这个东西是恍恍惚惚的。那样地惚惚恍恍,其中却有形象;那样地恍恍惚惚,其中却有实物。那样地深远暗昧,其中却有精质;这精质是非常真实的,这精质是可信验的。

从当今上溯到古代,它的名字永远不能消去,依据它才能认识万物的本始。我怎么知道万物本始的情形呢!从“道”认识的。

Chapter 21

Such the scope of the All-pervading Power.
That it alone can act through the Way.
For the Way is a thing impalpable, incommensurable.
Incommensurable, impalpable.
Yet latent in it are forms;
Impalpable, incommensurable
Yet within it are entities.
Shadowy it is and dim;
Yet within it there is a force,[1]
A force that though rarefied
Is none the less efficacious.
From the time of old till now
Its charge has not departed
But cheers onward the many warriors.
How do I know that the many warriors are so?
Through this[2].

第二十二章

【原文】

曲则全,枉则直,
洼则盈,敝则新,
少则得,多则惑。
是以圣人抱一为天下式。
不自见,故明;
不自是,故彰;
不自伐,故有功;
不自矜,故长。
夫唯不争,故天下莫能与之争。
古之所谓"曲则全"者,
岂虚言哉!
诚全而归之。

【今译】

委曲反能保全,屈就反能伸展,低洼反能充盈,敝旧反能生新,少取反能多得,贪多反而迷惑。

所以有道的人坚守这一原则作为天下事理的范式。不自我表扬,反能显明;不自以为是,反能彰显;不自己夸耀,反能见功;不自我矜持,反能长久。

正因为不跟人争,所以天下没有人和他争。古人所说的"委曲可以保全"等话,怎么会是空话呢!它是实实在在能够达到的。

Chapter 22

"To remain whole, be twisted!"

To become straight, let yourself be bent.

To become full, be hollow.

Be tattered, that you may be renewed.

Those that have little, may get more,

Those that have much, are but perplexed.

Therefore the Sage

Clasps the Primal Unity,

Testing by it everything under heaven.

He does not show himself; therefore he is seen everywhere.

He does not define himself, therefore he is distinct.

He does not boast of what he will do, therefore he succeeds.

He is not proud of his work, and therefore it endures.

He does not contend,

And for that very reason no one under heaven can contend with him.

So then we see that the ancient saying "To remain whole, be twisted!" was no idle word; for true wholeness can only be achieved by return.[1]

第二十三章

【原文】

希言自然。

故飘风不终朝,骤雨不终日。孰为此者?天地。天地尚不能久,而况于人乎?

故从事于"道"者,同于"道";"德"者,同于"德";失者,同于失。同于"道"者,"道"亦乐得之;同于"德"者,"德"亦乐得之;同于失者,失亦乐得之。

信不足焉,有不信焉。

【今译】

不言教令是合于自然的。

所以狂风刮不到一早晨,暴雨下不了一整天。谁使它这样的?是天地。天地的狂暴都不能持久,何况人呢?

所以从事于"道"的,就同于"道";从事"德"的,就同于"德";表现失"道"失"德"的,行为就是暴戾恣肆。同于"道"的人,"道"也乐于得到他;同于"德"的,"德"也乐于得到他;同于失"道"失"德"的,就会得到失"道"失"德"的后果。

统治者的诚信不足,人民自然不相信他。

Chapter 23

To be always talking is against nature.

For the same reason a hurricane never lasts a whole morning, nor a rainstorm all day. Who is it that makes the wind and rain? It is Heaven-and-Earth[1].

And if even Heaven-and-Earth cannot blow or pour for long, how much less in his utterance should man?

Truly, if one uses the Way as one's instrument, the results will be like the Way; if one uses the "power" as one's instrument, the results will be like the "power". If one uses what is the reverse of the "power"[2], the results will be the reverse of the "power".

For to those who have conformed themselves to the Way, the Way readily lends its power. To those who have conformed themselves to the power, the power readily lends more power. While to those who conform themselves to inefficacy, inefficacy readily lends its ineffectiveness.

"It is by not believing in people that your turn them into liars."[3]

第二十四章

【原文】

企者不立；
跨者不行；
自见者不明；
自是者不彰；
自伐者无功；
自矜者不长。
其在道也，
曰：余食赘形。
物或恶之，
故有道者不处。

【今译】

踮起脚跟，是站不牢的；跨步前进，是走不远的；自逞己见的，反而不得自明；自以为是的，反而不得彰显；自己夸耀的，反而不得见功；自我矜持的，反而不得长久。

从“道”的观点来看，这些急躁炫耀的行为，可说都是剩饭赘瘤。惹人厌恶，所以有“道”的人不这样做。

Chapter 24

"He who stands on tip-toe, does not stand firm;

He who takes the longest strides, does not walk the fastest."

He who does his own looking sees little,[1]

He who defines himself is not therefore distinct.

He who boasts of what he will do succeeds in nothing;

He who is proud of his work, achieves nothing that endures.

Of these, from the standpoint of the Way, it is said,

"Pass round superfluous dishes to those that have already had enough.

And no creature but will reject them in disgust."

That is why he that possesses Tao does not linger.[2]

第二十五章

【原文】

有物混成，先天地生。
寂兮寥兮，
独立而不改，
周行而不殆，
可以为天地母。
吾不知其名，
强字之曰“道”，
强为之名曰“大”。
大曰逝，逝曰远，远曰反。
故“道”大，
天大，地大，人亦大。
域中有四大，
而人居其一焉。
人法地，地法天，天法“道”，“道”法自然。

【今译】

有一个浑然一体的东西，在天地形成以前就存在。听不见它的声音也看不着它的形体，它独立长存而永不衰竭，循环运行而生生不息，可以为天地万物的根源。我不知道它的名字，勉强叫它作“道”，再勉强给它起个名字叫作“大”。它广大无边而周流不息，周流不息而伸展遥远，伸展遥远而返回本源。

所以说,“道”大,天大,地大,人也大。宇宙间有四大,而人是四大之一。

人取法地,地取法天,天取法“道”,“道”纯任自然。

Chapter 25

There was something formless yet complete,
That existed before heaven and earth;
Without sound, without substance,
Dependent on nothing, unchanging,
All pervading, unfailing.

One may think of it as the mother of all things under heaven.

Its true name we do not know;
"Way" is the by-name that we give it.
Were I forced to say to what class of things it belongs
I should call it Great (ta).
Now ta also means passing on,
And passing on means going far away,
And going far away means returning.[1]

Thus just as Tao[2] has "this greatness" and as earth has it and as heaven has it, so may the ruler[3] also have it.

Thus "within the realm there are four portions of greatness," and one belongs to the king.

The ways of men are conditioned by those of earth.
The ways of earth, by those of heaven.
The ways of heaven, by those of Tao, and the ways of Tao, by the Self-so.[4]

第二十六章

【原文】

重为轻根，
静为躁君。
是以君子终日行不离辎重。
虽有荣观，燕处超然。
奈何万乘之主，
而以身轻天下？
轻则失根，
躁则失君。

【今译】

厚重是轻浮的根本，静定是躁动的主帅。

因此君子整天行走不离开载重的车辆。虽然有华丽的生活，却安居泰然。为什么身为大国的君主，反而把自身看得比天下社稷还轻微呢？

轻率就失去了根本，躁动就失去了主体的地位。

Chapter 26

As the heavy must be the foundation of the light,
So quietness is lord and master of activity.
Truly, "A man of consequence though he travels all day
Will not let himself be separated from his baggage-wagon,
However magnificent the view,[1] he sits quiet and dispassionate."
How much less, then, must be the lord of ten thousand chariots
Allow himself to be lighter[2] than these he rules!
If he is light, the foundation is lost;
If he is active, the lord and master[3] is lost.[4]

第二十七章

【原文】

善行无辙迹；
善言无瑕谪；
善数不用筹策；
善闭无关楗而不可开；
善结无绳约而不可解。
是以圣人常善救人，故无弃人；
常善救物，故无弃物。
是谓袭明。
故善人者，不善人之师；
不善人者，善人之资。
不贵其师，
不爱其资，
虽智大迷。
是故要妙。

【今译】

善于行走的，不留痕迹；善于言谈的，言辞没有差错；善于计算的，不用筹码；善于关闭的，不用栓销却使人不能开；善于捆缚的，不用绳索却使人不能解。

因此，有道的人经常善于做到人尽其才，所以没有被遗弃的人；经常善于做到物尽其用，所以没有被废弃的物。这就叫作保持明境。

所以善人可以做为不善人的老师，不善人为善人的借鉴。不尊重他的老师，不珍惜他的借鉴，虽然自以为聪明，其实是大迷糊。这真是个精要深奥的道理。

Chapter 27

Perfect activity[1] leaves no track behind it;

Perfect speech is like a jade-worker whose tool leaves no mark.

The perfect reckoner needs no counting-slips;[2]

The perfect door has neither bolt nor bar,

Yet cannot be opened.

The perfect knot needs neither rope nor twine,

Yet cannot be untied.

Therefore the Sage,

Is all the time in the most perfect way helping men,

He certainly does not turn his back on men;

Is all the time in the most perfect way helping creatures,

He certainly does not turn his back on creatures.

This is called resorting to the Light.[3]

Truly, "the perfect man is the teacher of the imperfect;

But the imperfect is the stock-in-trade of the perfect man."[4]

He who does not respect his teacher,

He who does not take care of his stock-in-trade,

Much learning though he may possess, is far astray.

This[5] is the essential secret.

第二十八章

【原文】

知其雄，守其雌，
为天下溪。
为天下溪，常德不离，
复归于婴儿。
知其白，（守其黑，
为天下式。
为天下式，常德不忒，
复归于无极。
知其荣，）守其辱，
为天下谷。
为天下谷，常德乃足，
复归于朴。
朴散则为器，圣人用之，
则为官长，
故大制不割。

【今译】

深知雄强，却安于雌柔，作为天下的溪涧。作为天下的溪涧，常"德"就不会离失，而回复到婴儿的状态。

深知明亮，（却坚守黑暗，作为检验万物的准则。坚持这一准则，常"德"就不会出错，而回归到无限的状况。深知荣耀，）却安于暗昧，作为天下的川谷。作为天下的川谷，常“德”才可以充足，而回复到真朴的状态。

真朴的“道”分散成万物，有道的人沿用真朴，则为百官的首长。所以完善的政治是不割裂的。

Chapter 28

"He who knows the male, yet cleaves to what is female
Becomes like a ravine, receiving all things under heaven,"
And being such a ravine
He knows all the time a power that he never calls upon in vain.
This is returning to the state of infancy.
He who knows the white, (yet cleaves to the black
Becomes the standard by which all things are tested;
And being such a standard
He has all the time a power that never errs,
He returns to the Limitless.
He who knows glory,)[1] yet cleaves to ignominy
Becomes like a valley that receives into it all things under heaven,
And being such a valley
He has all the time a power that suffices;
He returns to the state of the Uncarved Block.
Now when a block is sawed up it is made into implements;[2]
But when the Sage uses it, it becomes Chief of all Ministers.
Truly, "The greatest carver[3] does the least cutting."

第二十九章

【原文】

将欲取天下而为之，
吾见其不得已。
天下神器，
不可为也，
（不可执也。）
为者败之，
执者失之。
（是以圣人无为，故无败；无执，故无失。）
夫物或行或随；
或歔或吹；
或强或羸；
或载或隳。
是以圣人去甚，
去奢，去泰。

【今译】

想要治理天下却用强力去做，我看他不能达到目的了。“天下”是神圣的东西，不能出于强力，（不能加以把持。）出于强力的，一定会失败；加以把持的，一定会失去。（因此圣人不妄为，所以不会失败；不把持，所以不会失去。）

世人（秉性不一）有前行，有后随，有响暖，有吹寒；有刚强，有羸弱；有安定，有危险。

因此圣人要去除极端的、奢侈的、过度的措施。

Chapter 29

Those that would gain what is under heaven by tampering with it—I have seen that they do not succeed.

For that which is under heaven is like a holy vessel,[1] dangerous to tamper with.

(And impossible to grab at.)[2]

Those that tamper with it, harm it.

Those that grab at it, lose it.

(Therefore the Sage does not act,

And as a result, he doesn't ruin things;

He does not hold on to things,

And as a result, he doesn't lose things.)[3]

For among the creatures of the world[4] some go in front, some follow;

Some blow hot when others would be blowing cold.

Some are feeling vigorous just when others are worn out.

Some are loading just when others would be tilting out.

Therefore the Sage "discards the absolute, the all-inclusive, the extreme."[5]

第三十章

【原文】

以道佐人主者,不以兵强天下。其事好还。师之所处,荆棘生焉。大军之后,必有凶年。

善有果而已,不敢以取强。果而勿矜,果而勿伐,果而勿骄,果而不得已,果而勿强。

物壮则老,是谓不道,不道早已。

【今译】

用道辅助君主的人,不靠兵力逞强于天下。用兵这件事一定会得到还报。军队所到的地方,荆棘就长满了。大战过后,一定会变成荒年。

善用兵的只求达到救济危难的目的就是了,不敢用兵来逞强。达到目的却不矜持,达到目的却不夸耀,达到目的却不骄傲,达到目的却出于不得已,达到目的却不逞强。

凡是气势壮盛的就会趋于衰败,这是不合于道的,不合于道很快就会消逝。

Chapter 30

He who by Tao purposes to help a ruler of men
Will oppose all conquest by force of arms;
For such things are wont to rebound.[1]
Where armies are, thorn and brambles grow.
The raising of a great host
Is followed by a year of dearth.

Therefore a good general effects his purpose and then stops; he does not take further advantage of his victory.

Fulfils his purpose and does not glory in what he has done;
Fulfils his purpose and does not boast of what he has done;
Fulfils his purpose, but takes no pride in what he has done;
Fulfils his purpose, but only as a step that could not be avoided.
Fulfils his purpose, but without violence;
For what has a time of vigour also has a time of decay.
This is against Tao,
And what is against Tao will soon perish.

第三十一章

【原文】

夫兵者，不祥之器，物或恶之，故有道者不处。

君子居则贵左，用兵则贵右。兵者不祥之器，非君子之器，不得已而用之，恬淡为上。胜而不美，而美之者，是乐杀人。夫乐杀人者，则不可得志于天下矣。

吉事尚左，凶事尚右。偏将军居左，上将军居右。言以丧礼处之。杀人之众，以悲哀泣之，战胜以丧礼处之。

【今译】

兵革是不祥的东西，大家都厌恶它，所以有道的人不使用它。

君子平时以左方为贵，用兵时以右方为贵。兵革是不祥的东西，不是君子所使用的东西。万不得已而使用它，最好要淡然处之。胜利了也不要得意洋洋，如果得意洋洋，就是喜欢杀人。喜欢杀人的，就不能实现统治天下的愿望啦。

吉庆的事情以左方为上，凶丧的事情以右方为上。偏将军在左边，上将军在右边，这是说出兵打仗用丧礼的仪式来处理。杀人众多，带着哀痛的心情去参加，打了胜仗要用丧礼的仪式去处理。

Chapter 31

Fine weapons[1] are none the less ill-omened things. (People despise them, therefore, those in possession of the Tao do not depend on them.)[2] That is why, among people of good birth, in peace the left-hand side is the place of honour, but in war this is reversed and the right-hand side is the place of honour. (Weapons are ill-omened things, which the superior man should not depend on. When he has no choice but to use them, the best attitude is to remain tranquil and peaceful.)[3] The Quietist, even when he conquers, does not regard weapons as lovely things. For to think them lovely means to delight in them, and to delight in them means to delight in the slaughter of men. And he who delights in the slaughter of men will never get what he looks for out of those that dwell under heaven. (Thus in happy events, the left-hand is the place of honour, in grief and mourning, the right-hand is the place of honour. The lieutenant general stands on the left, while the supreme general stands on the right, which is arranged on the rites of mourning.)[4] A host that has slain men is received with grief and mourning; he that has conquered in battle is received with rites of mourning.

第三十二章

【原文】

“道”常无名、朴。
虽小,天下莫能臣。
侯王若能守之,
万物将自宾。
天地相合,
以降甘露,
民莫之令而自均。
始制有名,
名亦既有,
夫亦将知止,
知止可以不殆。
譬“道”之在天下,
犹川谷之于江海。

【今译】

“道”永远是无名而又好像未经雕琢的素材。(它的呈现)虽然幽微(不可见),天下却没有人能不臣服于它。侯王如果能守住它,万物将会自然地归从。

天地间(阴阳之气)相合,就降下甘露,人们不需指使它而自然均匀。万物兴作就产生了各种名称,各种名称已经制定了,就知道有个限度,知道有所限度,就可以避免危险。

“道”存在于天下,有如江海为河川所流注一样。

Chapter 32

Tao is eternal, but has no fame (name);
The Uncarved Block, though seemingly of small account,
Is greater than anything that is under heaven.[1]
If kings and barons would but possess themselves of it,
The ten thousand creatures would flock to do them homage;
Heaven-and-Earth would conspire
To send Sweet Dew,
Without law or compulsion, men would dwell in harmony.[2]
Once the block is carved, there will be names,
And so soon as there are names
Know that it is time to stop.
Only by knowing when it is time to stop can danger be avoided.
To Tao[3] all under heaven will come
As streams and torrents flow into a great river or sea.

第三十三章

【原文】

知人者智,自知者明。
胜人者有力,自胜者强。
知足者富。
强行者有志。
不失其所者久。
死而不亡者寿。

【今译】

认识别人的是机智,了解自己的才算高明。
战胜别人的是有力,克服自己的才算刚强。
知道满足的就是富有。
努力不懈的就是有志。
不迷失本性的就能长久。
身死而不被遗忘的是真正的长寿。

Chapter 33

To understand others is to have knowledge;
To understand oneself is to be illumined.
To conquer others needs strength;
To conquer oneself is harder still.
To be content with what one has is to be rich.
He that works through violence[1] may get his way;
But only what stays in its place
Can endure.
When one dies one is not lost, there is no other longevity.

第三十四章

【原文】

大道汜兮,其可左右。
万物恃之以生而不辞,
功成而不有。
衣养万物而不为主,
(常无欲,)可名为小;
万物归焉而不为主,
可名为大。
以其终不自为大,
故能成其大。

【今译】

大道广泛流行,无所不到。万物依赖它生长而不推辞,有所成就而不自以为有功。养育万物而不自以为主,可以称它为“小”;万物归附而不自以为主宰,可以称它为“大”。由于它不自以为伟大,所以才能成就它的伟大。

Chapter 34

Great Tao is like a boat that drifts;

It can go this way; it can go that.[1]

The ten thousand creatures owe their existence to it and it does not disown them;

Yet having produced them, it does not take possession of them.

Tao, though it covers the ten thousand things like a garment,[2]

Makes no claim to be master over them,

(And asks for nothing from them.)[3]

Therefore it may be called the Lowly.

The ten thousand creatures obey it,

Though they know not that they have a master;

Therefore it is called the Great.

So too the Sage just because he never at any time makes a show of greatness in fact achieves greatness.

第三十五章

【原文】

执大象,天下往。
往而不害,安平太。
乐与饵,过客止。
"道"之出口,淡乎其无味,
视之不足见,听之不足闻,
用之不足既。

【今译】

执守大"道",天下人都会归附他。会归附他而不互相伤害,于是大家都平和安泰。

音乐和美食,能使过路的人停步。而"道"的表述,却淡得没有味道,看它却看不见,听它却听不着,用它却用不完。

Chapter 35

He who holding the Great Form[1] goes about his work in the empire

Can go about his work, yet do no harm.

All is peace, quietness and security.[2]

Sound of music, smell of good dishes

Will make the passing stranger pause.

How different the words that Tao gives forth!

So thin, so flavourless!

If one looks for Tao, there is nothing solid to see;

If one listens for it, there is nothing loud enough to hear.

Yet if one uses it, it is inexhaustible.

第三十六章

【原文】

将欲歙之,必固张之;
将欲弱之,必固强之;
将欲废之,必固兴之;
将欲取之,必固与之。
是谓微明。
柔弱胜刚强。
鱼不可脱于渊,
国之利器不可以示人。

【今译】

将要收敛的,必先扩张;将要削弱的,必先加强;将要废弃的,必先兴举;将要夺取的,必先给予。这就是深沉的预见。

柔弱胜过刚强。鱼不能离开深渊,国家的"利器"不可以随便耀示于人。

Chapter 36

What is in the end to be shrunk
Must first be stretched.
Whatever is to be weakened
Must begin by being made strong.
What is to be overthrown
Must begin by being set up.
He who would be a taker
Must begin as a giver.
This is called "dimming" one's light.[1]
It is thus that the soft overcomes the hard
And the weak, the strong.
"It is best to leave the fish down in his pool;
Best to leave the State's sharpest weapons[2] where none can see them."[3]

第三十七章

【原文】

“道”常无为而无不为。
侯王若能守之，
万物将自化。
化而欲作，
吾将镇之以无名之朴。
镇之以无名之朴，
夫将不欲。
不欲以静，
天下将自正。

【今译】

“道”永远是顺任自然的，然而没有一件事不是它所为。侯王如果能够持守它，万物就会自生自长。自生自长而至贪欲萌作时，我就用“道”的真朴来镇住它。用“道”的真朴来镇住它，就不会起贪欲。不起贪欲而归于安静，天下自然走上正常的轨道。

Chapter 37

Tao never does;
Yet through it all things are done.
If the barons and kings would but possess themselves of it,
The ten thousand creatures would at once be transformed.[1]
And if having been transformed they should desire to act,
We must restrain them by the blankness[2] of the Unnamed.
The blankness of the Unnamed[3]
Brings dispassion;[4]
To be dispassionate is to be still.
And so,[5] of itself, the whole empire will be at rest.

第三十八章

【原文】

上“德”不德，是以有“德”；
下“德”不失德，是以无“德”。
上“德”无为而无以为；下“德”无为而有以为。
上仁为之而无以为；上义为之而有以为。
上礼为之而莫之应，则攘臂而扔之。
故失“道”而后“德”，失“德”而后仁，
失仁而后义，失义而后礼。
夫礼者，忠信之薄，而乱之首。
前识者，“道”之华，而愚之始。
是以大丈夫处其厚，
不居其薄；
处其实，不居其华。
故去彼取此。

【今译】

上“德”的人不自恃有德，所以真正是有“德”；下“德”的人自以为不离失德，所以没有达到“德”。

上“德”的人顺任自然而无心作为；下“德”的人顺任自然而有心作为。

上仁的人有所作为却出于无意；上义的人有所作为且出于有意。

上礼的人有所作为而得不到回应，于是就扬着胳膊使人强从。

所以失去了“道”而后才有“德”，失去了“德”而后才有仁，失去了仁而后才有义，失去了义而后才有礼。

礼是忠信的不足，而祸乱的开端。

所谓“先知”，不过是“道”的虚华，是愚昧的开始。

因此大丈夫立身敦厚，而不居于浇薄；存心笃实，而不居于虚华。所以舍弃薄华而采取厚实。

Chapter 38

The man of highest "power" does not reveal himself as a possessor of "power";

Therefore he keeps his "power".

The man of inferior "power" cannot rid it of the appearance of "power";

Therefore he is in truth without "power".

The man of highest "power" neither acts[1] nor is there any who so regards him;[2]

The man of inferior "power" both acts and is so regarded.

The man of highest humanity, though he acts, is not so regarded;

Whereas a man of even the highest morality both acts and is so regarded;

While even he who is best versed in ritual not merely acts, but if people fail to respond

Then he will pull up his sleeves and advance upon them.

That is why it is said,

"After Tao was lost, then came the 'power';

After the 'power' was lost, then came human kindness.

After human kindness was lost, then came morality,

After morality was lost, then came ritual.

Now ritual is the mere husk of loyalty and promise-keeping

And is indeed the first step towards brawling."[3]

Foreknowledge may be the "flower of doctrine",

But it is the beginning of folly.

Therefore the full-grown man[4] takes his stand upon the solid substance and not upon the mere husk,

Upon the fruit and not upon the flower.

Truly, "he rejects that and takes this."

第三十九章

【原文】

昔之得“一”者：
天得“一”以清；地得“一”以宁；
神得“一”以灵；谷得“一”以盈；
万物得“一”以生；侯王得“一”以为天下正。
其致之也，谓天无以清，将恐裂；
地无以宁，将恐废；神无以灵，将恐歇；
谷无以盈，将恐竭；万物无以生，将恐灭；
侯王无以正，将恐蹶。
故贵以贱为本，高以下为基。
是以侯王自称孤、寡、不榖。
此非以贱为本邪？非乎？故至誉无誉。
是故不欲琭琭如玉，珞珞如石。

【今译】

从来凡是得到“一”的——天得到“一”而清明；地得到“一”而宁静；神得到“一”而灵妙；河谷得到“一”而充盈；万物得到“一”而生长；侯王得到“一”而使得天下安定。

推而言之，天不能保持清明，难免要崩裂；地不能保持宁静，难免要震溃；神不能保持灵妙，难免要消失；河谷不能保持充盈，难免要涸竭；万物不能保持生长，难免要绝灭；侯王不能保持清静，难免要颠覆。

所以贵以贱为根本，高以下为基础。

因此侯王自称为“孤”、“寡”、“不榖”。这不是把低贱当作根本吗？岂不是吗？所以最高的称誉是无须夸誉的。因此不愿像玉的华丽，宁可如石块般的坚实。

Chapter 39

As for the things that from of old have understood the Whole——

The sky through such understanding remains limpid,

Earth remains steady,

The spirits keep their holiness,

The abyss is replenished,

The ten thousand creatures bear their kind,

Barons and princes direct their people.

It is the Whole that causes it.

Were it not so limpid, the sky would soon get torn,

Were it not for steadiness, the earth would soon tip over,

Were it not for their holiness, the spirits would soon wither away,

Were it not for this replenishment, the abyss would soon go dry,

Were it not that the ten thousand creatures can bear their kind,

They would soon become extinct.

Were the barons and princes no longer directors of their people and for that reason honoured and exalted, they would soon be overthrown.

Truly, "the humble is the stem upon which the mighty grows, the low is the foundation upon which the high is laid."

That is why barons and princes refer to themselves as "The Orphan", "The Needy", "The Ill-provided".[1]

Is this not indeed a case of might rooting itself upon humility?

True indeed are the sayings:

"Enumerate the parts of a carriage, and you still have not explained what a carriage is,"[2] and "They[3] did not want themselves to tinkle like jade-bells, while others resounded like stonechimes."[4]

第四十章

【原文】

反者“道”之动；
弱者“道”之用。
天下万物生于“有”，
“有”生于“无”。

【今译】

“道”的运动是循环的；“道”的作用是柔弱的。

天下万物生于“有”，“有”生于“无”。

Chapter 40

In Tao the only motion is returning;

The only useful quality, weakness.

For though all creatures under heaven are the products of Being,

Being itself is the product of Not-being.[1]

第四十一章

【原文】

上士闻道，勤而行之；中士闻道，若存若亡；下士闻道，大笑之。

不笑不足以为道。

故建言有之：

明道若昧；进道若退；

夷道若颣；上德若谷；

广德若不足；建德若偷；

质真若渝；大白若辱；

大方无隅；大器晚成；

大音希声；大象无形；

“道”隐无名。

夫唯“道”，善贷且成。

【今译】

上等士人听了“道”，努力去实行；中等士人听了“道”，将信将疑；下等士人听了“道”，哈哈大笑。——不被嘲笑，那就不足以成为“道”！所以古时候立言的人说过这样的话：

光明的道好似暗昧；前进的道好似后退；

平坦的道好似崎岖；崇高的德好似低下的川谷；

广大的德好似不足；刚健的德好似懈怠的样子；

质朴而纯真好似浑浊的样子；最洁白的好像含垢的

样子；

最方正的反而没有棱角；贵重的器物总是最后完成；

最大的乐声反而听来无音响；

最大的形象反而看不见形迹；

“道”幽隐而没有名称。

只有“道”，善于辅助万物。

Chapter 41

When the man of highest capacities hears Tao
He does his best to put it into practice.
When the man of middling capacity hears Tao
He is in two minds about it.
When the man of low capacity hears Tao
He laughs loudly at it.
If he did not laugh, it would not be worth the name of Tao.
Therefore the proverb has it:
"The way[1] out into the light often looks dark,
The way that goes ahead often looks as if it went back."
The way that is least hilly often looks as if it went up and down,
The "power" that is really loftiest looks like an abyss,
What is sheerest white looks blurred.[2]
The "power" that is most sufficing looks inadequate,
The "power" that stands firmest looks flimsy.
What is in its natural, pure state looks faded;
The largest square has no corners,
The greatest vessel takes the longest to finish,
Great music has the faintest notes,
The Great Form is without shape.
For Tao is hidden and nameless.
Yet Tao alone supports all things and brings them to fulfilment.

第四十二章

【原文】

“道”生一，
一生二，
二生三，
三生万物。
万物负阴而抱阳，
冲气以为和。
（人之所恶，
唯孤、寡、不穀，
而王公以为称。
故物或损之而益，
或益之而损。
人之所教，
我亦教之。
强梁者不得其死，
吾将以为教父。）

【今译】

“道”是独一无偶的，独一无偶的“道”禀负阴阳两气，阴阳两气相交而成一种适匀的状态，万物都在这种状态中产生的。万物背阴而向阳，阴阳两气互相激荡而成新的和谐体。

（人所厌恶的就是“孤”、“寡”、“不穀”，但是王公却用来称呼自己。所以一切事物，减损它有时反而得到增加，增加它有时反而受到减损。别人教导我的，我也用来教导人。强暴的人不得好死，我把它当作施教的根本。）

Chapter 42

Tao gave birth to the One; the One gave birth successively to two things, three things, up to ten thousand.[1] These ten thousand creatures cannot turn their backs to the shade without having the sun on their bellies,[2] and it is on this blending of the breaths that their harmony depends.

(To be orphaned, needy, ill-provided[3] is what men most hate; yet princes and dukes style themselves so. Truly, "things are often increased by seeking to diminish them and diminished by seeking to increase them." The maxims that others use in their teaching I too will use in mine. Show me a man of violence that came to a good end, and I will take him for my teacher.)[4]

第四十三章

【原文】

天下之至柔，
驰骋天下之至坚。
无有入无间，
吾是以知无为之有益。
不言之教，
无为之益，
天下希及之。

【今译】

天下最柔软的东西，能战胜天下最坚硬的东西。无形的力量能穿透没有间隙的东西，我因此知道“无为”的益处。

“不言”的教导，“无为”的益处，天下很少能够做得到的。

Chapter 43

What is of all things most yielding
Can overwhelm that which is of all things most hard.
Being substanceless it can enter even where there is no space;
That is how I know the value of action that is actionless.
But that there can be teaching without words,
Value in action that is actionless,
Few indeed can understand.

第四十四章

【原文】

名与身孰亲?
身与货孰多?
得与亡孰病?
甚爱必大费;
多藏必厚亡。
故知足不辱,
知止不殆,
可以长久。

【今译】

声名和生命比起来哪一样亲切?生命和财富比起来哪一样贵重?得到名利和丧失生命哪一样更有害?

过分的爱名就必定要付出重大的耗费;丰富的藏货就必定会招致惨重的损失。

所以知道满足就不会受到屈辱,知道适可而止就不会带来危险,这样才可以保持长久。

Chapter 44

Fame or one's own self, which matters to one most?

One's own self or things bought, which should count most?

In the getting or the losing, Which is worse?[1]

Hence he who grudges expense pays dearest in the end;[2]

He who has hoarded most will suffer the heaviest loss.

Be content with what you have and are, and no one can despoil you;

Who stops in time nothing can harm.

He is forever safe and secure.

第四十五章

【原文】

大成若缺,其用不敝。
大盈若冲,其用不穷。
大直若屈,大巧若拙,
大辩若讷。
静胜躁,寒胜热。
清净为天下正。

【今译】

最完满的东西好像有欠缺一样,但是它的作用是不会衰竭的。

最充盈的东西好像是空虚一样,但是它的作用是不会穷尽的。

最正直的东西好像是弯曲一样,
最灵巧的东西好像是笨拙一样,
最卓越的辩才好像是口讷一样。

清净克服扰动,寒冷克服暑热。清净无为可以做人民的模范。

Chapter 45

What is most perfect seems to have something missing;
Yet its use is unimpaired.
What is most full seems empty;
Yet its use will never fail.
What is most straight seems crooked;
The greatest skill seems like clumsiness,
The greatest eloquence like stuttering.
Movement overcomes cold;
But staying still overcomes heat. [1]
So he by his limpid calm
Puts right everything under heaven. [2]

第四十六章

【原文】

天下有道，
却走马以粪。
天下无道，
戎马生于郊。
（罪莫大于可欲。）
祸莫大于不知足；
咎莫大于欲得。
故知足之足，
常足矣。

【今译】

国家政治清平，把战马还给农夫用来耕种。国家政治混乱，连怀胎的母马也要用来作战。

（罪过没有比诱人贪求更大的了。）

祸患没有比过于不知足更大的了；罪过没有比过于贪得无厌更大的了。所以知道满足为止的人，永远是满足的。

Chapter 46

When there is Tao in the empire

The galloping steeds are turned back to fertilize the ground by their droppings.

When there is not Tao in the empire

War horses will be reared even on the sacred mounds below the city walls.

(No lure is greater than to possess what others want,)[1]

No disaster greater than not to be content with what one has,

No presage of evil greater than that men should be wanting to get more.

Truly: "He who has once known the contentment that comes simply through being content, will never again be otherwise than contented."

第四十七章

【原文】

不出户，知天下；
不窥牖，见天道。
其出弥远，
其知弥少。
是以圣人不行而知，
不见而明，不为而成。

【今译】

不出门外，能够推知天下的事理；不望窗外，能够了解自然变化的规律。他越向外奔逐，而他所知的理也越少。

所以有道的人不必经历就能知情，不必眼见就能心明，不必作为却能成功。

第四十七章

Chapter 47

Without leaving his door
He knows everything under heaven.
Without looking out of his window
He knows all the ways of heaven.
For the further one travels[1]
The less one knows.
Therefore the Sage arrives without going,
Sees all without looking,
Does nothing, yet achieves everything.

第四十八章

【原文】

为学日益，
为道日损。
损之又损，
以至于无为。
取天下常以无事，
及其有事，
不足以取天下。

【今译】

求学一天比一天增加(知见)，求道一天比一天减少(情欲)。减少又减少，一直到“无为”的境地。

如能不妄为那就没有什么事情做不成的了。治理国家要常清静不扰攘，一旦生事时，就不配治理国家了。

Chapter 48

Learning consists in adding to one's stock day by day;
The practice of Tao consists in "substracting day by day,
Substracting and yet again substracting
Till one has reached inactivity.[1]
But by this very inactivity
Everything can be activated."

Those who of old won the adherence of all who live under heaven
All did so by not interfering.
Had they interfered,
They would never have won this adherence.

第四十九章

【原文】

圣人常无心，
以百姓心为心。
善者，吾善之；
不善者，吾亦善之；
德善。
信者，吾信之；
不信者，吾亦信之；
德信。
圣人在天下，歙歙焉，
为天下浑其心，
百姓皆注其耳目，
圣人皆孩之。

【今译】

有道的人没有私心，以百姓的心为心。

善良的人，我善待他；不善良的人，我也善待他；这样可使人人向善。

守信的人，我信任他；不守信的人，我也信任他；这样可使人人守信。

有道的人在位，收敛自己的意欲，使人心思化归于浑厚淳朴，百姓都专注他们自己的耳目，有道的人使他们都回复到婴孩般（真纯）的状态。

Chapter 49

The Sage has no heart[1] of his own;

He uses the heart of the people as his heart.

Of the good man I approve,

But of the bad I also approve,

And thus he gets goodness.

The truthful man I believe, but the liar I also believe,

And thus he gets truthfulness.

The Sage, in his dealings with the world, seems like one dazed with fright;

For the world's sake he dulls his wits.

The Hundred Families[2] all the time strain their eyes and ears,

The Sage all the time sees and hears no more than an infant sees and hears.[3]

第五十章

【原文】

出生入死。
生之徒,十有三;
死之徒,十有三;
人之生,动之于死地,
亦十有三。
夫何故?
以其生生之厚。
盖闻善摄生者,
陆行不遇兕虎,
入军不被甲兵;
兕无所投其角,
虎无所用其爪,
兵无所用其刃。
夫何故,以其无死地。

【今译】

人出世为“生”,入地为“死”。属于长寿的,占十分之三;属于短命的,占十分之三;本来可以活得长久,却自己走向死路的,也占了十分之三。为什么呢?因为他们迫切要求生存,反而达不到目的。听说善于养护生命的人,在陆地上行走不会遇到犀牛和老虎,在战争中不会受到杀伤;犀牛用不上它的角,老虎用不上它的爪,兵器用不上它的刃。为什么呢?因为他没有进入死亡的范围。

Chapter 50

He who aims at life achieves death.[1]

If the "companions of life" are thirteen,[2] so likewise are the "companions of death" thirteen.

How is it that the "death-spots" in man's life and activity are also thirteen?[3]

It is because men feed life too grossly.

It is said that he who has a true hold on life, when he walks on land does not meet tigers or wild buffaloes;[4] in battle he is not touched by weapons of war.

Indeed, a buffalo that attacked him would find nothing for its horns to butt, a tiger would find nothing for its claws to tear, a weapon would find no place for its point to enter in.

And why?

Because such men have no "death-spots" in them.

第五十一章

【原文】

“道”生之,“德”畜之,物形之,势成之。

是以万物莫不尊“道”而贵“德”。

“道”之尊,“德”之贵,夫莫之命而常自然。

故“道”生之,“德”畜之;长之育之;亭之毒之;养之覆之。生而不有,为而不恃,长而不宰。是为“玄德”。

【今译】

“道”生成万物,“德”畜养万物,万物呈现各种形态,环境使万物成长。

所以万物没有不尊崇“道”而珍贵“德”的。

“道”之所以受尊崇,“德”之所以被珍贵,就在于对它不加干涉,而顺任自然。

所以“道”生成万物,“德”畜养万物;使万物成长发育;使万物成熟结果;对万物抚养调护。生长万物却不据为己有,兴作万物却不自恃己能,使万物滋长而不加以主宰。这就是最深的“德”。

Chapter 51

Tao gave them birth;

The "power" of Tao reared them,

Shaped them according to their kinds,

Perfected them, giving to each its strength.[1]

Therefore of the ten thousand things there is not one that does not worship Tao and do homage to its "power". No mandate even went forth that accorded to Tao the right to be worshipped, nor to its "power" the right to be worshipped, nor to its "power" the right to receive homage.

It was always and of itself so.

Therefore as Tao bore them and the "power" of Tao reared them, made them grow, fostered them, harboured them, brewed[2] for them, so you must

"Rear them, but not lay claim to them,

Control them,[3] but never lean upon them,

Be chief among them, but not manage them.

This is called the mysterious power."[4]

第五十二章

【原文】

天下有始，以为天下母。既得其母，以知其子；既知其子，复守其母，没身不殆。

塞其兑，闭其门，终身不勤。开其兑，济其事，终身不救。

见小曰明，守柔曰强。用其光，复归其明，无遗身殃；是为袭常。

【今译】

天地万物都有本始，作为天地万物的根源。如果得知根源，就能认识万物；如果认识万物，又持守着万物的根源，终身都没有危险。

塞住嗜欲的孔窍，闭起嗜欲的门径，终身都没有劳扰的事。打开嗜欲的孔窍，增添纷杂的事件，终身都不可救治。

能察见细微的叫作“明”，能持守柔弱的叫作“强”。运用智慧的光，返照内在的“明”，不给自己带来灾殃；这叫作永续不绝的常“道”。

Chapter 52

That which was the beginning of all things under heaven
We may speak of as the "mother" of all things.
He who apprehends the mother[1]
Thereby knows the sons.[2]
And he who has known the sons,
Will hold all the tighter to the mother,
And to the end of his days suffer no harm:
"Block the passages, shut the doors,
And till the end your strength shall not fail.
Open up the passages, increase your doings,
And till your last day no help shall come to you."
As good sight means seeing what is very small
So strength means holding on to what is weak.[3]
He who having used the outer-light can return to the inner-light
Is thereby preserved from all harm.
This is called resorting to the always-so.

第五十三章

【原文】

使我介然有知，行于大道。
唯施是畏。
大道甚夷，
而人好径。
朝甚除，
田甚芜，
仓甚虚；
服文采，
带利剑，厌饮食，财货有余；
是谓盗夸。非道也哉！

【今译】

假使我稍微有些认识，在大道上行走，担心唯恐走入了邪路。

大道很平坦，但是人君却喜欢走险僻的小路。宫殿十分整洁，农田非常荒芜，仓库十分空虚；还穿着锦绣的衣服，佩带锋利的宝剑，饱足精美的饮食，搜括足余的财货；这就叫作强盗头子。多么的无道啊！

Chapter 53

He who has the least scrap of sense, once he has got started on the great highway has nothing to fear so long as he avoids turning. For great highways are safe and easy.

But men love by-paths. [1]

So long as the Court is in order[2]

They are content to let their fields run to weed

And their granaries stand empty.

They wear patterns and embroideries,

Carry sharp swords, glut themselves with drink and food, have more possessions than they can use.

These are the riotous ways of brigandage; they are not the Highway.

第五十四章

【原文】

善建者不拔,善抱者不脱,子孙以祭祀不辍。
修之于身,其德乃真;
修之于家,其德乃余;
修之于乡,其德乃长;
修之于邦,其德乃丰;
修之于天下,其德乃普。
故以身观身,以家观家,
以乡观乡,以邦观邦,
以天下观天下。
吾何以知天下然哉?
以此。

【今译】

善于建树的不会中途动摇,善于保持的不会脱落,如果子孙能遵行这个道理,则世世代代的祭祀不会断绝。

拿这个道理贯彻到个人,他的“德”是会真实的;贯彻到一家,他的“德”可以有余;贯彻到一乡,他的“德”能受尊崇;贯彻到一国,他的“德”就会昌盛;贯彻到天下,他的“德”就会普遍。

所以要从(我)个人观照(其他的)个人,从(我)家观照(其他人的)家,从(我的)乡观照(其他的)乡,从(我的)国观照(其他的)国,从(我的)天下观照(其他的)天下。我怎么知道天下的情况呢?就是用这种道理。

Chapter 54

What Tao[1] plants cannot be plucked,

What Tao clasps, cannot slip.

By its virtue alone can one generation after another carry on the ancestral sacrifice.[2]

Apply it to yourself and by its power you will be freed from dross.

Apply it to your household and your household shall thereby have abundance.

Apply it to the village, and the village will be made secure.

Apply it to the kingdom, and the kingdom shall thereby be made to flourish.

Apply it to an empire, and the empire shall thereby be extended.

Therefore just as through[3] oneself one may contemplate Oneself,

So through the household one may contemplate the Household[4],

And through the village, one may contemplate the Village,

And through the kingdom, one may contemplate the Kingdom,

And through the empire, one may contemplate the Empire.

How do I know that the empire is so?

By this.

第五十五章

【原文】

含“德”之厚，比于赤子。
毒虫不螫，猛兽不据，
攫鸟不搏。
骨弱筋柔而握固。
未知牝牡之合而朘作，
精之至也。
终日号而不嗄，
和之至也。
知和曰“常”，
知常曰“明”。
益生曰祥。
心使气曰强。
物壮则老，
谓之不道，
不道早已。

【今译】

含“德”深厚的人，比得上初生的婴儿。毒虫不刺伤他，猛兽不伤害他，凶鸟不搏击他。他筋骨柔弱，拳头却握得很牢固。他还不知道男女交合但小生殖器却常常勃起，这是精气充足的缘故。他整天号哭，但是他的喉咙却不会沙哑，这是元气醇和的缘故。

认识醇和的道理叫作“常”，认识“常”叫作“明”。贪生纵欲就会灾殃，欲念主使和气就是逞强。过分的强壮就趋于衰老，这叫作不合于“道”，不合于“道”很快就会死亡。

Chapter 55

The impunity of things[1] fraught with the "power"
May be likened to that of an infant.
Poisonous insects do not sting it,
Nor fierce beasts seize it,
Nor clawing birds maul it.
Its bones are soft, its sinews weak; but its grip is strong.
Not yet to have known the union of male and female, but to be completely formed,
Means that the vital force is at its height;
To be able to scream all day without getting hoarse
Means that the harmony is at its perfection.
To understand such harmony is to understand the always-so.
To understand the always-so is to be illumined[2]
But to fill life to the brim is to invite omens.
If the heart makes calls upon the life-breath, rigidity follows.
Whatever has a time of vigour also has a time of decay.
Such things are against Tao,
And whatever is against Tao is soon destroyed.

第五十六章

【原文】

知者不言，
言者不知。
（塞其兑，
闭其门；）
挫其锐，
解其纷，
和其光，
同其尘，
是为“玄同”。
故不可得而亲，
不可得而疏；
不可得而利，
不可得而害；
不可得而贵，
不可得而贱。
故为天下贵。

【今译】

智者是不会夸夸其谈的，夸夸其谈的人就不是智者。

（塞住嗜欲的孔窍，闭起嗜欲的门径；）不露锋芒，消解纷扰，含敛光耀，混同尘世，这就是玄妙齐同的境界。这样就不分亲，不分疏；不分利，不分害；不分贵，不分贱。所以为天下人所尊贵。

Chapter 56

Those who know do not speak;
Those who speak do not know.
(Block the passages,
Shut the doors,)[1]
Let all sharpness be blunted,
All tangles untied,
All glare tempered.
All dust smoothed.
This is called the mysterious levelling.[2]

He who has achieved it cannot either be drawn into friendship or repelled,

Cannot be benefited, cannot be harmed,
Cannot either be raised or humbled,

And for that very reason is highest of all creatures under heaven.

第五十七章

【原文】

以正治国,以奇用兵,以无事取天下。
吾何以知其然哉?
以此:
天下多忌讳,而民弥贫;
人多利器,国家滋昏;
人多伎巧,奇物滋起;
法令滋彰,盗贼多有。
故圣人云:“我无为,
而民自化;
我好静,而民自正;
我无事,而民自富;
我无欲,而民自朴。”

【今译】

以正大光明的方法治国,以诡奇的方法用兵,以不搅扰人民来治理天下。我怎么知道是这样的?从下面这些事端上可以看出:

天下的禁忌越多,人民越陷于贫困;人间的利器越多,国家越陷于昏乱;人们的技巧越多,邪恶的事情就连连发生;法令越森严,盗贼反而不断地增加。

所以有道的人说:“我无为,人民就自然顺化;我好静,人民就自然上轨道;我不搅扰,人民就自然富足;我没有贪欲,人民就自然朴实。”

Chapter 57

"Kingdoms can only be governed if rules are kept;

Battles can only be won if rules are broken."[1]

But the adherence of all under heaven can only be won by letting-alone.

How do I know that it is so?

By this.[2]

The more prohibition there are, the more ritual avoidances,

The poorer the people will be.

The more "sharp weapons" there are,

The more benighted will the whole land grow.

The more cunning craftsmen there are,

The more pernicious contrivances will be invented.

The more laws are promulgated,

The more thieves and bandits there will be.

Therefore a sage has said,

So long as I "do nothing" the people will of themselves be transformed.

So long as I love quietude, the people will of themselves go straight.

So long as I act only by inactivity the people will of themselves become prosperous.

So long as I have no wants the people will of themselves return to the "state of the Uncarved Block."

第五十八章

【原文】

其政闷闷，其民淳淳；
其政察察，其民缺缺。
祸兮，福之所倚；
福兮，祸之所伏。
孰知其极？其无正也。
正复为奇，善复为妖。
人之迷，其日固久。
是以圣人方而不割，
廉而不刿，
直而不肆，
光而不耀。

【今译】

政治宽厚，人民就纯朴；政治严苛，人民就狡黠。

灾祸啊，幸福倚傍在它里面；幸福啊，灾祸藏伏在它之中。谁知道它们的究竟？它们并没有一个定准！正忽而转变为邪，善忽而转变为恶。人们的迷惑，已经有长久的时日了。

因而有道的人方正而不割人，锐利而不伤人，直率而不放肆，光亮而不耀目。

Chapter 58

When the ruler looks depressed the people will be happy and satisfied;[1]

When the ruler looks lively and self-assured the people will be carping and discontented.

"It is upon bad fortune that good fortune leans, upon good fortune that bad fortune rests."

But though few know it, there is a bourn where there is neither right nor wrong;

In a realm where every straight is doubled by a crooked, and every good by an ill, surely mankind has gone long enough astray?

Therefore the Sage
Squares without cutting,
Shapes the corners without lopping,
Straightens without stretching,
Gives forth light without shining.[2]

第五十九章

【原文】

治人事天，莫若啬。
夫唯啬，是谓早服；
早服谓之重积德；
重积德则无不克；
无不克则莫知其极；
莫知其极，
可以有国；
有国之母，可以长久；
是谓深根固柢，
长生久视之道。

【今译】

治理国家，养护身心，没有比爱惜精力更重要。

爱惜精力，乃是早作准备；早作准备就是不断地积“德”；不断地积德就没有什么不能胜任的；没有什么不能胜任就无法估计他的力量；无法估计他的力量，就可以担负保护国家的责任；掌握治理国家的道理，就可以长久维持；这就是根深柢固、“长生久视”的道理。

Chapter 59

You cannot rule men nor serve heaven[1] unless you have laid up a store;[2]

This "laying up a store" means quickly absorbing,

And "quickly absorbing" means doubling one's garnered "power".

Double your garnered power and it acquires a strength that nothing can overcome.

If there is nothing it cannot overcome, it knows no bounds,

And only what knows no bounds is huge enough to keep a whole kingdom in its grasp.

But only he who having the kingdom goes to the Mother can keep it long.

This[3] is called the art of making the roots strike deep by fencing the trunk, of making life long by fixed staring.[4]

第六十章

【原文】

治大国,若烹小鲜。
以道莅天下,其鬼不神;
非其鬼不神,其神不伤人;
非其神不伤人,圣人亦不伤人。
夫两不相伤,故德交归焉。

【今译】

治理大国,好像煎小鱼。

用“道”治理天下,鬼怪起不了作用;不但鬼怪起不了作用,神祇也不侵越人;不但神祇不侵越人,圣人也不侵越人。鬼神和有道者都不侵越人,所以彼此能相安无事。

Chapter 60

Ruling a large kingdom is indeed like cooking small fish.

They who by Tao ruled all that is under heaven did not let an evil spirit within them display its powers. Nay, it was not only that the evil spirit did not display its powers; neither was the Sage's good[1] spirit used to the hurt of other men. Nor was it only that his good spirit was not used to harm other men, the Sage himself was thus saved from harm.[2] And so, each being saved from harm, their "powers" could converge towards a common end.

第六十一章

【原文】

大邦者下流，
天下之牝，
天下之交也。
牝常以静胜牡，
以静为下。
故大邦以下小邦，
则取小邦；
小邦以下大邦，
则取大邦。
故或下以取，
或下而取。
大邦不过欲兼畜人，
小邦不过欲入事人。
夫两者各得所欲，
大者宜为下。

【今译】

大国要像居于江河的下流，处在天下雌柔的位置，是天下交汇的地方。雌柔常以静定而胜过雄强，因为静定而又能处下的缘故。

所以大国对小国谦下，就可以汇聚小国；小国对大国谦下,就可以见容(于大国)。所以有时(大国)谦下以汇聚(小国),有时(小国)谦下而见容于大国。大国不过要聚养小国,小国不过要求见容于大国。这样大国小国都可以达到愿望。大国尤其应该谦下。

Chapter 61

A large kingdom must be like the low ground towards which all streams flow down. It must be a point towards which all things under heaven converge. Its part must be that of the female in its dealings with all things under heaven.[1]

The female by quiescence conquers the male; by quiescence gets underneath. If a large kingdom can in the same way succeed in getting underneath a small kingdom then it will win the adherence of the small kingdom; and it is because small kingdoms are by nature in this way underneath large kingdoms that they win the adherence[2] of large kingdoms. The one must get underneath in order to do it; the other is underneath and therefore does it. (What large countries really need is more inhabitants; and what small countries need is some place where their surplus inhabitants can go and get employment.)[3] Thus each gets what it needs. That is why I say the large kingdom must "get underneath".

第六十二章

【原文】

道者万物之奥。
善人之保，
不善人之所保。
美言可以市尊，
美行可以加人。
人之不善，
何弃之有？
故立天子，
置三公，
虽有拱璧以先驷马，
不如坐进此道。古之所以贵此道者何？
不曰求以得，
有罪以免邪？
故为天下贵。

【今译】

“道”是万物的归宿。善人珍贵它，不善的人也处处保住它。

（得“道”的善人）嘉美的言词可以博人尊敬，良好的行为可以见重于人。不善的人，怎能把“道”舍弃呢？所以立位天子，设置三公，虽然敬奉拱璧在先、驷马在后的礼仪，还不如用"道"来作为献礼。

古时候重视"道"的原因是什么呢？岂不是说有求的就可以得到，有罪的就可以免除吗？所以被天下人所贵重。

Chapter 62

Tao in the Universe is like the southwest corner in the house. [1]

It is the treasure of the good man,

The support of the bad.

There is a traffic in speakers of fine words;

Persons of grave demeanour are accepted as gifts;

Even the bad let slip no opportunity to acquire them.

Therefore on the day of an Emperor's enthronement

Or at the installation of the three officers[2] of State

Rather than send a team of four horses, preceded by a disc of jade,

Better were it, as can be done without moving from one's seat, to send this Tao.

For what did the ancients say of this Tao, how did they prize it? Did they not say of those that have it "Pursuing, they shall catch; pursued, they shall escape"? They thought it, indeed, most precious of all things under heaven.

第六十三章

【原文】

为无为,事无事,味无味。

大小多少,(报怨以德。)图难于其易,为大于其细;天下难事,必作于易,天下大事,必作于细。是以圣人终不为大,故能成其大。

夫轻诺必寡信,多易必多难。是以圣人犹难之,故终无难矣。

【今译】

以无为的态度去作为,以不搅扰的方式去作事,以恬淡无味当作味。

大生于小,多起于少,(用德来报答怨恨。)处理困难要从容易的入手,实现远大要从细微的入手;天下的难事,必定从容易的做起;天下的大事,必定从细微的做起。所以有道的人始终不自以为大,因此能成就大的事情。

轻易允诺的信用一定不足;把事情看得太容易时遭遇的困难一定更多。所以有道的人遇见事情总是把它看得艰难,因此终究没有困难了。

Chapter 63

It acts without action, does without doing, finds flavour in what is flavourless,

Can make the small great and the few many,[1]

(Requites injuries with good deeds,)[2]

Deals with the hard while it is still easy,

With the great while it is still small.

In the governance of empire everything difficult must be dealt with while it is still easy,

Everything great must be dealt with while it is still small.

Therefore the Sage never has to deal with the great; and so achieves greatness.

But again "Light assent inspires little confidence

And 'many easies' means many a hard."

Therefore the Sage knows too how to make the easy difficult, and by doing so avoid all difficulties!

第六十四章

【原文】

其安易持,其未兆易谋。其脆易泮,其微易散。
为之于未有,治之于未乱。
合抱之木,生于毫末;
九层之台,起于累土;
千里之行,始于足下。
(为者败之,执者失之。
是以圣人无为故无败;无执故无失。)
民之从事,常于几成而败之。
慎终如始,则无败事。
(是以圣人欲不欲,不贵难得之货;
学不学,复众人之所过,以辅万物之自然而不敢为。)

【今译】

局面安稳时容易持守,事变没有迹象时容易图谋。事物脆弱时容易消解,事物微细时容易散失。要在事情没有发生以前就处理妥当,要在祸乱没有产生以前就早作准备。

合抱的大木,是从细小的萌芽生长起来的;九层的高台,是从一堆泥土建筑起来的;千里的远行,是从脚下举步开始走出来的。

(出于强力的,一定会失败;加以把持的,一定会失去。因此圣人不妄为,所以不会失败;不把持,所以不会失去。)

人们做事情,常常在快要成功的时候就失败了。事情要完成的时候也能像开始的时候一样的谨慎,那就不会败事了。

(所以有道的人意欲别人所不意欲的,不珍贵难得的货品;有道的人学别人所不学的,挽救众人的过错,以辅助万物的自然发展而不加以干预。)

Chapter 64

What stays still is easy to hold;

Before there has been an omen it is easy to lay plans.

What is tender is easily torn,

What is minute is easy to scatter.

Deal with things in their state of not-yet-being,

Put them in order before they have got into confusion.

For "the tree big as a man's embrace began as a tiny sprout,

The tower nine storeys high began with a heap of earth,

The journey of a thousand leagues began with what was under the feet."

(He who acts, harms; he who grabs, lets slip.

Therefore the Sage does not act, and so does not harm;

Does not grab, and so does not let slip.)[1]

Whereas the people of the world, at their tasks,

Constantly spoil things when within an ace of completing them.

Heed the end no less than the beginning,

And your work will not be spoiled.

(Therefore the Sage wants only things that are unwanted,

Sets no store by products difficult to get,

And so teaches things untaught,

Turning all men back to the things they have left behind,

That the ten thousand creatures may be restored to their Self-so.

This he does; but dare not act.)[2]

第六十五章

【原文】

古之善为道者，
非以明民，
将以愚之。
民之难治，
以其智多。
故以智治国，
国之贼；
不以智治国，
国之福。
如此两者亦稽式。
常知稽式，
是谓“玄德”，
“玄德”深矣，远矣，
与物反矣，
然后乃至大顺。

【今译】

从前善于行道的人，不是教人民精巧，而是使人民淳朴。

人民所以难治，乃是因为他们使用太多的智巧心机。所以用智巧去治理国家，是国家的灾祸；不用智巧去治理国家，是国家的幸福。

了解这两种治国方式的差别就是一个法则。经常认识这个法则,就是“玄德”,“玄德”好深好远啊!和事物复归到真朴,然后顺应于自然。

Chapter 65

In the days of old those who practised Tao with success did not, by means of it, enlighten the people, but on the contrary sought to make them ignorant.

The more knowledge people have, the harder they are to rule.

Those who seek to rule by giving knowledge
Are like bandits preying on the land.
Those who rule without giving knowledge
Bring a stock of good fortune to the land.

To have understood the difference between these two things is to have a test and standard[1]

To be always able to apply this test and standard
Is called the mysterious "power",
The mysterious "power", so deep-penetrating,
So far-reaching,
That can follow things back—
All the way back to the Great Concordance.

第六十六章

【原文】

江海之所以能为百谷王者，
以其善下之，
故能为百谷王。
是以圣人欲上民，
必以言下之；
欲先民，
必以身后之。
是以圣人处上而民不重，
处前而民不害。
是以天下乐推而不厌。
以其不争，
故天下莫能与之争。

【今译】

江海所以能成为许多河流汇往的地方，因为它善于处在低下的地位，所以能成为许多河流所汇往。

所以“圣人”要成为人民的领导，必须心口一致地对他们谦下；要作为人民的表率，必须把自己的利益放在人民的后面。所以“圣人”居于上位而人民不感到负累；居于前面而人民不感到受害。所以天下人民乐于推戴而不厌弃。因为他不跟人争，所以天下没有人能和他争。

Chapter 66

How did the great rivers and seas get their kingship over the hundred lesser streams?

Through the merit of being lower than they; that was how they got their kingship.

Therefore the Sage

In order to be above the people

Must speak as though he were lower than the people.

In order to guide them

He must put himself behind them.

Only thus can the Sage be on top and the people not be crushed by his weight.

Only thus can he guide, and the people not be led into harm.

Indeed in this way everything under heaven will be glad to be pushed by him[1] and will not find his guidance irksome. This he does by not striving; and because he does not strive, none can contend with him.

第六十七章

【原文】

（天下皆谓我："'道'大，似不肖。"夫唯大，故似不肖。若肖，久矣其细也夫！）

我有三宝，持而保之。一曰慈，二曰俭，三曰不敢为天下先。

慈故能勇；俭故能广；不敢为天下先，故能成器长。

今舍慈且勇；舍俭且广；舍后且先；死矣！

夫慈，以战则胜，以守则固。天将救之，以慈卫之。

【今译】

（天下人都对我说："'道'广大，却不像任何具体的东西。"正因为它的广大，所以不像任何具体的东西。如果它像的话，早就渺小了。）

我有三种宝贝，持守而保全着。第一种叫作慈爱，第二种叫作俭啬，第三种叫作不敢居于天下人的前面。

慈爱所以能勇武；俭啬所以能宽广；不敢居于天下人的前面，所以能成为万物的首长。

现在舍弃慈爱而求取勇武；舍弃俭啬而求取宽广；舍弃退让而求取争先，是走向死路！

慈爱，用来征战就能胜利，用来守卫就能巩固。天要救助谁，就用慈爱来卫护他。

Chapter 67

(Every one under heaven says that our Way is greatly like folly. But it is just because it is great, that it seems like folly. As for things that do not seem like folly—well, there can be no question about their smallness!)[1]

Here are my three treasures.[2] Guard and keep them! The first is pity; the second, frugality; the third, refusal to be "foremost of all things under heaven".

For only he that pities is truly able to be brave;
Only he that is frugal is truly able to be profuse.
Only he that refuses to be foremost of all things
Is truly able to become chief of all Ministers.[3]

At present your bravery is not based on pity, nor your profusion on frugality, nor your vanguard on your rear; and this is death. But pity cannot fight without conquering or guard without saving. Heaven arms with pity those whom it would not see destroyed.[4]

第六十八章

【原文】

善为士者，不武；
善战者，不怒；
善胜敌者，不与；
善用人者，为之下。
是谓不争之德，
是谓用人之力，
是谓配天古之极。

【今译】

善作将帅的，不逞勇武；善于作战的，不轻易激怒；善于战胜敌人的，不用对斗；善于用人的，对人谦下。这叫作不争的“德”，这叫作运用别人的能力，这叫作符合于自然的道理。

Chapter 68

The best charioteers do not rush ahead;[1]
The best fighters do not make displays of wrath.
The greatest conqueror wins without joining issue;
The best user of men acts as though he were their inferior.
This is called the power that comes of not contending,
Is called the capacity to use men,
The secret of being mated to heaven, to what was of old.

第六十九章

【原文】

用兵有言：
“吾不敢为主，而为客；
不敢进寸而退尺。”
是谓行无行；攘无臂；
扔无敌；执无兵。
祸莫大于轻敌，
轻敌几丧吾宝。
故抗兵相若，
哀者胜矣。

【今译】

用兵的曾说：“我不敢进犯，而采取守势；不敢前进一寸，而要后退一尺。”这就是说：虽然有阵势，却像没有阵势可摆；虽然要奋臂，却像没有臂膀可举；虽然面临敌人，却像没有敌人可赴；虽然有兵器，却像没有兵器可持。

祸患没有再比轻敌更大的了，轻敌几乎丧失了我的“三宝”。

所以，两军对阵兵力相当的时候，悲哀的一方可获得胜利。

Chapter 69

The strategists have the sayings: "When you doubt[1] your ability to meet the enemy's attack, take the offensive yourself," and "If you doubt[2] your ability to advance an inch, then retreat a foot."

This latter is what we call to march without moving,

To roll the sleeve, but present no bare arm,[3]

The hand that seems to hold, yet had no weapon in it,

A host that can confront, yet presents no battle-front.[4]

Now the greatest of all calamities is to attack and find no enemy.

I can have no enemy only at the price of losing my treasure.[5]

Therefore when armies are raised and issues joined it is he who does not delight in war that wins.

第七十章

【原文】

吾言甚易知,甚易行。
天下莫能知,莫能行。
言有宗,事有君。
夫唯无知,是以不我知。
知我者希,则我者贵。
是以圣人被褐而怀玉。

【今译】

我的话很容易了解,很容易实行。大家却不能明白,不能实行。

言论有主旨,行事有根据。正由于不了解这个道理,所以不了解我。

了解我的人越少,取法我的人就很难得了。因而有道的圣人穿着粗衣而内怀美玉。

Chapter 70

My words are very easy to understand and very easy to put into practice. Yet no one under heaven understands them; no one puts them into practice. But my words have an ancestry, my deeds have a lord;[1] and it is precisely because men do not understand this that they are unable to understand me.

Few then understand me; but it is upon this very fact that my value depends.[2] It is indeed in this sense that "the Sage wears hair-cloth[3] on top, but carries jade underneath his dress."

第七十一章

【原文】

知不知,尚矣;
不知知,病也。
圣人不病,
以其病病。
夫唯病病,
是以不病。

【今译】

知道自己有所不知道,最好;不知道却自以为知道,这是缺点。有道的人没有缺点,因为他把缺点当作缺点。正因为他把缺点当作缺点,所以他是没有缺点的。

Chapter 71

To know when one does not know is best.

To think one knows when one does not know is a dire disease.

"Only he who recognizes this disease as a disease[1]

Can cure himself of the disease."[2]

The sage's way of curing disease

Also consists in making people recognize their diseases as diseases and thus ceasing to be diseased.

第七十二章

【原文】

民不畏威，则大威至。
无狎其所居，无厌其所生。
夫唯不厌，是以不厌。
是以圣人自知不自见；
自爱不自贵。故去彼取此。

【今译】

人民不畏惧统治者的威压，那么更大的祸乱就要发生了。

不要逼使人民不得安居，不要压榨人民的生活。只有不压榨人民，人民才不厌恶（统治者）。

因此，有道的人但求自知而不自我表扬；但求自爱而不显高贵。所以舍去后者而取前者。

Chapter 72

Never mind if the people are not intimidated by your authority. A Mightier Authority[1] will deal with them in the end.[2] Do not narrow their dwellings or harass their lives;[3] and for the very reason that you do not harass them, they will cease to turn from you. Therefore the Sage knows himself but does not show himself. Knows his own value, but does not put himself on high. Truly, "he rejects that but takes this."

第七十三章

【原文】

勇于敢则杀,勇于不敢则活。
此两者,或利或害。
天之所恶,孰知其故?
(是以圣人犹难之。)
天之道,不争而善胜,
不言而善应,
不召而自来,
绰然而善谋。
天网恢恢,疏而不失。

【今译】

勇于坚强就会死,勇于柔弱就可活。这两种勇的结果,有的得利,有的遭害。天道所厌恶的,谁知道是什么缘故?

(圣人对此也难以了解。)

自然的规律,是不争让而善于得胜,不说话而善于回应,不召唤而自动来到,宽缓而善于筹策。自然的范围广大无边,稀疏而不会有一点漏失。

Chapter 73

He whose braveness lies in daring, slays.
He whose braveness lies in not daring, gives life.
Of these two, either may be profitable or unprofitable.[1]
But "Heaven hates what it hates;
None can know the reason why."
(Wherefore the Sage, too, disallows it.)[2]

For it is the way of Heaven not to strive but none the less to conquer,

Not to speak, but none the less to get an answer,

Not to beckon; yet things come to it of themselves.

Heaven is like one who says little, yet none the less has laid his plans.

Heaven's net is wide;
Coarse are the meshes, yet nothing slips through.

第七十四章

【原文】

民不畏死，奈何以死惧之？
若使民常畏死，而为奇者，
吾得执而杀之，孰敢？
常有司杀者杀。
夫代司杀者杀，
是谓代大匠斫。
夫代大匠斫者，
希有不伤其手矣。

【今译】

人民不畏惧死亡，为什么用死亡来恐吓他？如果使人民真的畏惧死亡，对于为邪作恶的人，我们就可以把他抓来杀掉，谁还敢为非作歹？

经常有专管杀人的去执行杀的任务。那代替专管杀人的去执行杀的任务，这就如同代替木匠去砍木头一样。那代替木匠砍木头的，很少有不砍伤自己手的。

Chapter 74

The people are not frightened of death. What then is the use of trying to intimate them with the death-penalty?

And even supposing people were generally frightened of death and did not regard it as an everyday thing,[1] which of us would dare to seize them and slay them?

There is the Lord of Slaughter[2] always ready for this task, and to do it in his stead is like thrusting oneself into the master-carpenter's place and doing his chipping for him. Now "he who tries to do the master-carpenter's chipping for him is lucky if he does not cut his hand."[3]

第七十五章

【原文】

民之饥,以其上食税之多,是以饥。
民之难治,以其上之有为,是以难治。
民之轻死,以其上求生之厚,是以轻死。
夫唯无以生为者,是贤于贵生。

【今译】

人民之所以饥饿,就是由于统治者吃税太多,因此陷于饥饿。

人民之所以难治,就是由于统治者强作妄为,因此难以管治。

人民之所以轻死,就是由于统治者过分追求享受,因此轻于犯死。

只有不求一己私利的人,要胜过自我奉养奢厚的人。

Chapter 75

The people starve because those above them eat too much tax-grain. That is the only reason why they starve.

The people are difficult to keep in order because those above them interfere. That is the only reason why they are so difficult to keep in order.

The people attach no importance to death, because those above them are too grossly absorbed in the pursuit of life. That is why they attach no importance to death.

And indeed, in that their hearts are so little set on life they are superior to those who set store by life.

第七十六章

【原文】

人之生也柔弱,其死也坚强。

草木之生也柔脆,其死也枯槁。

故坚强者死之徒,柔弱者生之徒。

是以兵强则灭,木强则折。

强大处下,柔弱处上。

【今译】

人活着的时候身体是柔软的,死了的时候就变成僵硬了。

草木生长的时候形质是柔脆的,死的时候就变成干枯了。

所以坚强的东西属于死亡的一类;柔弱的东西属于生存的一类。

因此用兵逞强就会遭受灭亡,树木强大就会遭受砍伐。

凡是强大的,反而居于下位,凡是柔弱的,反而占在上面。

Chapter 76

When he is born, man is soft and weak; in death he becomes stiff and hard. The ten thousand creatures[1] and all plants and trees while they are alive are supple and soft, but when they are dead they become brittle and dry. Truly, what is stiff and hard is a "companion of death"; what is soft and weak is a "companion of life". Therefore "the weapon that is too hard will be broken,[2] the tree that has the hardest wood will be cut down." Truly, the hard and mighty are cast down; the soft and weak set on high.

第七十七章

【原文】

天之道,其犹张弓与?
高者抑之,下者举之;
有余者损之,不足者补之。
天之道,损有余而补不足。
人之道,则不然,损不足以奉有余。
孰能有余以奉天下,唯有道者。
(是以圣人为而不恃,
功成而不处,其不欲见贤。)

【今译】

自然的规律,岂不就像拉开弓弦一样吗?弦位高了,就把它压低,弦位低了就把它升高;有余的加以减少,不足的加以补充。自然的规律,减少有余,用来补充不足。社会的法规,就不是这样,却要剥夺不足,而用来供奉有余的人。

谁能够把有余的拿来供给天下不足的?这只有有道的人才能做到。

(因此有道的人作成万物而不自恃己能;有所成就而不以功自居,他不想表现自己的聪明才智。)

Chapter 77

Heaven's way is like the bending of a bow. When a bow is bent the top comes down and the bottom-end comes up. [1]

So too does Heaven take away from those who have too much, and give to those that have not enough. But if it is Heaven's way to take from those who have too much and give to those who have not enough, this is far from being man's way. He takes away from those that have not enough in order to make offering to those who already have too much. One there is and one only, so rich that he can afford to make offerings to all under heaven. Who is this? It is the possessor of Tao. (If, then, the Sage "though he controls does not lean, and when he has achieved his aim does not linger," it is because he does not wish to reveal himself as better than others.) [2]

第七十八章

【原文】

天下莫柔弱于水，
而攻坚强者莫之能胜，
以其无以易之。
弱之胜强，柔之胜刚，
天下莫不知，莫能行。
是以圣人云：
“受国之垢，是谓社稷主；
受国不祥，是谓天下王。”
正言若反。

【今译】

世间没有比水更柔弱的，冲激坚强的东西却没有能胜过它的，因为没有什么能代替它。

弱胜过强，柔胜过刚，天下没有人不知道，但是没有人能够实行。

因此有道的人说：“承担全国的屈辱，才配称国家的君主；承担全国的祸难，才配做天下的君王。”正面的话好像反话一样。

Chapter 78

Nothing under heaven is softer or more yielding than water; but when it attacks things hard and resistant there is not one of them that can prevail. For they can find no way of altering it.[1]

That the yielding conquers the resistant and the soft conquers the hard is a fact known by all men, yet utilized by none.

Yet it is in reference to this that the Sage said "Only he who has accepted the dirt of the country can be lord of its soil-shrines; only he who takes upon himself the evils of the country can become a king among those what dwell under heaven." Straight words seem crooked.[2]

第七十九章

【原文】

（报怨以德，）
和大怨，必有余怨；
安可以为善？
是以圣人执左契，
而不责于人。
有德司契，无德司彻。
天道无亲，常与善人。

【今译】

（用德来报答怨恨，）调解深重的怨恨，必然还有余留的怨恨；这怎能算是妥善的办法呢？

因此“圣人”保存借据的存根，但是并不向人索取偿还。有“德”的人只是管理借据（而不索债）；无“德”的人则实行税收（强行索取）。

自然的规律是没有偏爱的，经常帮助善良的人。

Chapter 79

(To requite injuries with good deeds.)[1]

To allay the main discontent, but only in a manner that will certainly produce further discontents can hardly be called successful.

Therefore the Sage behaves like the holder of the left-hand tally, who stays where he is and does not go round making claims on people.[2]

For he who has the "power" of Tao is the Grand Almoner; he who has not the "power" is the Grand Perquisitor. "It is Heaven's way, without distinction of persons, to keep the good perpetually supplied."

第八十章

【原文】

小国寡民。
使有什伯之器而不用;
使民重死而不远徙。
虽有舟舆,无所乘之;
虽有甲兵,无所陈之。
使民复结绳而用之。
甘其食,美其服,
安其居,乐其俗。
邻国相望,鸡犬之声相闻,
民至老死,不相往来。

【今译】

国土狭小人民稀少。即使有各种器具,却并不使用;使人民重视死亡而不向远方迁移。虽然有船只车辆,却没有必要去乘坐;虽然有铠甲武器,却没有机会去陈列。使人民回复到结绳记事的状况。

人民有甜美的饮食,美观的衣服,安适的居所,欢乐的习俗。邻国之间可以互相看得见,鸡鸣狗吠的声音可以相互听得着,人民从生到死,互相不往来。

Chapter 80

Given a small country with few inhabitants, he could bring it about that though there should be among the people contrivances requiring ten times, a hundred times less labour,[1] they would not use them. He could bring it about that the people would be ready to lay down their lives and lay them down again[2] in defence of their homes, rather than emigrate. There might still be boats and carriages, but no one would go in them; there might still be weapons of war but no one would drill with them. He could bring it about that "the people should have no use for any form of writing save knotted ropes, should be contented with their food, pleased with their clothing, satisfied with their homes, should take pleasure in their rustic tasks. The next place might be so near at hand that one could hear the cocks crowing in it, the dogs barking; but the people would grow old and die without ever having been there."[3]

第八十一章

【原文】

信言不美,美言不信。
善者不辩,辩者不善。
知者不博,博者不知。
圣人不积,既以为人己愈有,
既以与人己愈多。
天之道,利而不害;
人之道,为而不争。

【今译】

真实的言词不华美,华美的言词不真实。

行为善良的人不巧辩,巧辩的人不善良。

真正了解的人不广博,广博的人不能深入了解。

"圣人"不私自积藏,他尽量帮助别人,自己反而更充足;他尽量给与别人,自己反而更丰富。

自然的规律,利物而无害,人间的法则,施为而不争夺。

Chapter 81

True words are not fine-sounding;
Fine-sounding words are not true.
The good man does not prove by argument;
And he who proves by argument is not good.
True wisdom is different from much learning;
Much learning means little wisdom.
The Sage has no need to hoard;
When his own last scrap has been used up on behalf of others,
Lo, he has more than before!
When his own last scrap has been used up in giving to others,
Lo, his stock is even greater than before!
For heaven's way is to sharpen without cutting,[1]
And the Sage's way[2] is to act without striving.

附录 Appendixes

马王堆汉墓帛书《德道经》甲本 *

德 经

【·上德不德,是以有德。下德不失德,是以无】德。上德无【为而】无以为也。上仁为之【而无】以为也。上义为之而有以为也。上礼【为之而莫之应也,则】攘臂而乃(扔)之。故失道。失道矣而后德,失德而后仁,失仁而后义,【失】义而【后礼。夫礼者,忠信之薄也】,而乱之首也。【前识者,】道之华也,而愚之首也。是以大丈夫居其厚而不居其泊(薄),居其实不居其华。故去皮(彼)取此。昔之得一者,天得一以清,地得【一】以宁,神得一以霝(灵),浴【谷】得一以盈,侯【王得一】而以为正。其致之也,胃(谓)天毋已清将恐【裂】,胃(谓)地毋【已宁】将恐【发】,胃(谓)神毋已霝(灵)将恐歇,胃(谓)浴(谷)毋已盈将恐渴(竭),胃(谓)侯王毋已贵【以高将恐蹶】。故必贵而以贱为本,必高矣而以下为基。夫是以侯王自胃(谓)【曰】孤寡不橐(縠),此其贱【之本】与?非【也】?故致数与(誉)无与(誉)。是故不欲【禄禄】若玉,硌硌【若石】。【上士闻道,勤能行之。中士闻道,若存若亡。下士闻道,大笑之。弗笑,不足以为道。是以建言有之曰:明

* 马王堆汉墓帛书《德道经》甲本、乙本系由湖南省博物馆提供,原载《马王堆汉墓帛书(壹)》,文物出版社 1980 年 3 月出版。"【】"中的文字系缺损部分,由甲、乙两本互补,若两本俱残或彼此字数有出入时,则选用传世诸本补入。"·"系帛书甲本的分段符号。

道如费，进道如退，夷道如类。上德如榖，大白如辱，广德如不足。建德如偷，质真如渝，大方无隅。大器晚成，大音希声，大象无形，道褒无名。夫唯】道，善【始且善成。反也者】，道之动也。弱也者，道之用也。天【下之物生于有，有生于无。道生一，一生二，二生三，三生万物。万物负阴而抱阳】，中气以为和。天下之所恶，唯孤寡不橐（榖），而王公以自名也。勿（物）或敗（损）之【而益，益】之而敗（损）。故人【之所】教，夕（亦）议而教人。故强良（梁）者不得死，我【将】以为学父。天下之至柔，【驰】骋于天下之致（至）坚。无有入于无间。五（吾）是以知无为【之有】益也。不【言之】教，无为之益，【天】下希能及之矣。名与身孰亲？身与货孰多？得与亡孰病？甚【爱必大费，多藏必厚】亡。故知足不辱，知止不殆，可以长久。大成若缺，其用不幣（敝）。大盈若盅（冲），其用不竆（窘）。大直如诎（屈），大巧如拙，大赢如炳。趮（躁）胜寒，靓（静）胜炅（热）。请（清）靓（静），可以为天下正。·天下有道，【却】走马以粪。天下无道，戎马生于郊。·罪莫大于可欲，憠（祸）莫大于不知足，咎莫憯于欲得。【故知足之足】，恒足矣。不出于户，以知天下。不规（窥）于牖，以知天道。其出也弥远，其【知弥少。是以圣人不行而知，不见而名】，弗为而【成】。为【学者日益，闻道者日损。损之又损，以至于无为，无为而无不为。将欲】取天下也，恒【无事，及其有事也，又不足以取天下矣。圣人恒无心】，以百【姓】之心为【心】。善者善之，不善者亦善【之，得善也。信者信之，不信者亦信之，得】信也。【圣人】之在天下，愉愉焉，为天下浑心，百姓皆属耳目焉，圣人皆咳之。【出】生，【入死。生之徒十】有【三，死之】徒十有三，而民生生，动皆之死地之十有三。夫何故也？以其生生也。盖【闻善】执生者，陵行不【避】矢（兕）虎，入军不被甲兵。矢（兕）无所椯（揣）其角，虎无所昔（措）其蚤（爪），兵无所容【其刃，夫】何故也？以其无死地焉。·道生之而德畜之，物刑（形）之而器成之。是以万物尊道而贵【德。道】之尊，德之贵也，夫莫之时（爵）而恒自然也。·道生之，畜之，长之，遂之，亭之，□之，【养之，覆之。生而】弗有也，为而弗寺（恃）也，长而弗宰也，此之谓玄德。·天下有始，以为天下母。既（既）得其母，以知其【子】，复守其母，没身不殆。·塞其闆（闷），闭其门，终身不堇（勤）。启其闷，济其事，终身【不棘。见】小曰【明】，守柔曰强。用其光，复归其明。毋道（遗）身央（殃），是胃（谓）袭常。·使我擦（挈）有知也，【行于】大道，唯【施是畏。大道】甚夷，民甚好解。朝甚除，田甚芜，仓甚虚；服文采，带利【剑。厌】食，货【财有余。是谓盗夸。盗夸，非道也】。善建【者不】拔，【善抱者不脱】，子孙以祭祀【不绝。修之身，其德乃真。修之家，其德有】余。修之【乡，其德乃长，修之邦，其德乃丰。修之天下，其德乃溥】。以身【观】身，以家观家，以乡观乡，以邦观邦，以天【下】观【天下。吾何以知天下之然哉？以此。含德】之厚【者】，比于赤子。逢（蜂）㾗（蠆）蜾（虺）地（蛇）弗螫，攫鸟猛兽弗搏。骨弱筋柔而握固。未知牝牡【之会】而朘【怒】，精【之】至也。终曰（日）号而不发，和之至也。和曰常，知和<常>曰明，益生曰祥，心使气曰强。【物壮】即老，胃（谓）之不道，不【道早已。知者】弗言，言者弗知。塞其闷，闭其【门，和】其光，同其墊（尘），坐（挫）其阅（锐），解其纷，是胃（谓）玄同。故不可得而亲，亦不可得而疏；不可得而利，亦不可得而害；不可【得】而贵，亦不可得而浅（贱）。故为天下贵。·以正之（治）邦，以畸（奇）用兵，以无事取天下。吾何【以知其然】也戈（哉）？夫天下【多忌】讳，而民弥贫。民多利器，而邦家兹（滋）昏。人多知（智），而何（奇）物兹（滋）【起。法物滋章，而】盗贼【多有。是以圣人之言曰】：我无为也，而民自化。我好静，而民自正。我无事，民【自富。我欲不欲，而民自朴。其政闵闵,其邦屯屯】。其正(政)察察,其邦夬(缺)夬(缺)。懸(祸),福之所倚;福,懸(祸)之所伏;【孰知其极?其无正也?正复为奇,善复为妖。人之迷也,其日固久矣。是以方而不割,廉而不刺,直而不绁,光而不曜。治人事天,莫若啬。夫惟啬,是以早服。早服是谓重积德。重积德则无不克,无不克则莫知其极。莫知其极】,可以有国。有国之母,可以长久。是胃(谓)深槿(根)固氐(柢),长【生久视之】道也。【治大国若烹小鲜。以道莅】天下,其鬼不神。非其鬼不神也,其神不伤人也。非其申(神)不伤人也,圣人亦弗伤【也。夫两】不相【伤,故】德交归焉。大邦者,下流也,天下之牝。天下之郊(交)也,牝恒以靓(静)胜牡。为其靓(静)【也,故】宜为下。大邦【以】下小【邦】,则取小邦。小邦以下大邦,则取于大邦。故或下以取,或下而取。【故】大邦者不过欲兼畜人,小邦者不过欲入事人。夫皆得其欲,【故大邦者宜】为下。【道】者,万物之注也,善人之琛(宝)也,不善人之所琛(保)也。美言可以市,尊行可以贺(加)人。人之不善也,何弃【之】有?故立天子,置三卿,虽有共之璧以先驷马,不善〈若〉坐而进此。古之所以贵此者何也?不胃(谓)【求以】得,有罪以免舆(与)?故为天下贵。·为无为,事无事,味无未(味)。大小多少,报怨以德。图难乎【其易也,为大乎其细也】。天下之难作于易,天下之大作于细。是以圣人冬(终)不为大,故能【成其大。夫轻诺者必寡信。多易】必多难,是【以圣】人猷(犹)难之,故终于无难。·其安也,易持也。【其未兆也】,易谋【也。其脆也,易判也。其微也,易散也。为之于其未有,治之于其未乱也。合抱之木,生于】毫末。九成之台,作于羸(蔂)土。百仁(仞)之高,台(始)于足【下。为之者败之,执之者失之。圣人无为】也,【故】无败【也】;无执也,故无失也。民之从事也,恒于其成事而败之。故慎终若始,则【无败事矣。是以圣人】欲不欲,而不贵难得之肑（贼）；学不学，而复众人之所过；能辅万物之自【然，而】弗敢为。故曰：为道者非以明民也，将以愚之也。民之难【治】也，以其知（智）也。故以知（智）知邦，邦之贼也；以不知（智）知邦，【邦之】德也；恒知此两者，亦稽式也。恒知稽式，此胃（谓）玄德。玄德深矣，远矣，与物【反】矣，乃【至大顺。江】海之所以能为百浴（谷）王者，以其善下之，是以能为百浴（谷）王。是以圣人之欲上民也，必以其言下之；其欲先【民也】，必以其身后之。故居前而民弗害也，居上而民弗重也。天下乐隼（推）而弗猒（厌）也，非以其无静（争）与？故【天下莫能与】静（争）。·小邦寡（寡）民，使十百人之器毋用。使民重死而远送〈徙〉。有车周（舟）无所乘之，有甲兵无所陈【之。使民复结绳而】用之。甘其食，美其服，乐其俗，安其居。𨛫（邻）邦相壁〈望〉，鸡狗之声相闻，民【至老死不相往来。信言不美，美言】不【信。知】者不博，【博】者不知。善【者不多，多】者不善。·圣人无积，【既】以为【人，己愈有；既以予人，己愈多。故天之道，利而不害；人之道，为而弗争。天下皆谓我大，不肖】。夫唯【大】，故不宵（肖）。若宵（肖），细久矣。我恒有三葆（宝），之，一曰兹（慈），二曰检（俭），【三曰不敢为天下先。夫慈，故能勇；【俭】，故能广；不敢为天下先，故能为成事长。今舍其兹（慈），且勇；舍其后，且先；则必死矣。夫兹（慈），【以战】则胜，以守则固。天将建之，女（如）以兹（慈）垣之。善为士者不武，善战者不怒，善胜敌者弗【与】，善用人者为之下。【是】胃（谓）不静（争）之德，是胃（谓）用人，是胃（谓）天，古之极也。·用兵有言曰：吾不敢为主而为客，吾不进寸而芮（退）尺。是胃（谓）行无行，襄（攘）无臂，执无兵，乃（扔）无敌矣。𥝌（祸）莫于〈大〉于无適（敌），无適（敌）斤（近）亡吾葆（宝）矣。故称兵相若，则哀者胜矣。吾言甚易知也，甚易行也；而人莫之能知也，而莫之能行也。言有君，事有宗。夫唯无知也，是以不

【我知。知者希，则】我贵矣。是以圣人被褐而褱（怀）玉。知不知，尚矣；不知不知，病矣。是以圣人之不病，以其【病病。是以不病。民之不】畏畏（威），则大【威将至】矣。·母（毋）闸（狎）其所居，毋猒（厌）其所生。夫唯弗猒（厌），是【以不厌。是以圣人自知而不自见也，自爱】而不自贵也。故去被（彼）取此。·勇于敢者【则杀，勇】于不敢者则栝（活）。【知此两者，或利或害。天之所恶，孰知其故？天之道，不战而善胜】，不言而善应，不召而自来，弹（坦）而善谋。【天网恢恢，疏而不失。若民恒且不畏死】，奈何以杀愳（惧）之也？若民恒是〈畏〉死，则而为者吾将得而杀之，夫孰敢矣！若民【恒且】必畏死，则恒有司杀者。夫伐〈代〉司杀者杀，是伐〈代〉大匠斫也。夫伐〈代〉大匠斫者，则【希】不伤其手矣。·人之饥也，以其取食逆之多也，是以饥。百姓之不治也，以其上有以为【也】，是以不治。·民之巠（轻）死，以其求生之厚也，是以巠（轻）死。夫唯无以生为者，是贤贵生。·人之生也柔弱，其死也揎仞贤（坚）强。万物草木之生也柔脆，其死也椲（枯）槀（槁）。故曰："坚强者，死之徒也；柔弱微细，生之徒也。"兵强则不胜，木强则恒。强大居下，柔弱微细居上。天下【之道，犹张弓】者也，高者印（抑）之，下者举之，有余者敗（损）之，不足者补之。故天之道，敗（损）有【余而补不足；人之道则】不然，敗（损）【不足以】奉有余。孰能有余而有以取奉于天者乎？【唯有道者乎？是以圣人为而弗有，成功而弗居也。若此其不欲】见贤也。天下莫柔【弱于水，而攻】坚强者莫之能【先】也，以其无【以】易【之也。故柔胜刚，弱】胜强，天【下莫不知，而莫能】行也。故圣人之言云，曰：受邦之訽（诟），是胃（谓）社稷之主；受邦之不祥，是胃（谓）天下之王。【正言】若反。和大怨，必有余怨，焉可以为善？是以圣右介（契）而不以责于人。故有德司介（契），【无】德司𢼸（徹）。夫天道无亲，恒与善人。

道 经

·道,可道也,非恒道也。名,可名也,非恒名也。无名,万物之始也。有名,万物之母也。【故】恒无欲也,以观其眇(妙);恒有欲也,以观其所噭。两者同出,异名同胃(谓)。玄之有(又)玄,众眇(妙)之【门】。天下皆知美为美,恶已;皆知善,訾(斯)不善矣。有、无之相生也,难、易之相成也,长、短之相刑(形)也,高、下之相盈也,意〈音〉、声之相和也,先、后之相隋(随),恒也。是以声(圣)人居无为之事,行【不言之教。万物作而弗始】也,为而弗志(恃)也,成功而弗居也。夫唯居,是以弗去。不上贤,【使民不争。不贵难得之货,使】民不为【盗】。不【见可欲,使】民不乱。是以声(圣)人之【治也,虚其心,实其腹;弱其志】,强其骨。恒使民无知无欲也。使【夫知不敢弗为而已,则无不治矣。道冲,而用之又弗】盈也。潚(渊)呵始(似)万物之宗。锉(挫)其兑(锐),解其纷,和其光,同【其尘。湛呵似】或存。吾不知【谁】子也,象帝之先。天地不仁,以万物为刍狗。声(圣)人不仁,以百省(姓)【为刍】狗。天地【之】间,【其】犹橐籥舆(与)?虚而不淈(屈),踵(动)而俞(愈)出。多闻数穷,不若守于中。浴(谷)神【不】死,是胃(谓)玄牝。玄牝之门,是胃(谓)【天】地之根。绵绵呵若存,用之不堇(勤)。天长,地久。天地之所以能【长】且久者,以其不自生也,故能长生。是以声(圣)人芮(退)其身而身先,外其身而身存。不以其无【私】舆(与)?故能成其私。上善治(似)水。水善利万物而有静(争),居众之所恶,故几于道矣。居善地,心善潚(渊),予善信,正(政)善治,事善能,踵(动)善时。夫唯不静(争),故无尤。植(持)而盈之,不【若其已。揣而】□之□之,□可长葆之。金玉盈室,莫之守也。贵富而驕(骄),自遗咎也。功述(遂)身芮(退),天【之道也。戴营魄抱一,能毋离乎?槫气至柔】,能婴儿乎?脩(涤)除玄蓝(鉴),能毋疵乎？爱【民活国，能毋以知乎？天门启阖，能为雌乎？明白四达，能毋以为乎】？生之，畜之。生而弗【有，长而弗宰，是谓玄】德。卅【辐同一毂，当】其无【有，车】之用【也】。然（埏）埴为器，当其无有，埴器【之用也。凿户牖】，当其无有，【室】之用也。故有之以为利，无之以为用。五色使人目明〈盲〉，驰骋田腊（猎）使人【心发狂】，难得之價（货）使人之行方（妨），五味使人之口哺（爽），五音使人之耳聋。是以声（圣）人之治也，为腹不【为目】。故去罢（彼）耳〈取〉此。龙（宠）辱若惊，贵大梡（患）若身。苛（何）胃（谓）龙（宠）辱若惊？龙（宠）之为下，得之若惊，失【之】若惊，是胃（谓）龙（宠）辱若惊。何胃（谓）贵大梡（患）若身？吾所以有大梡（患）者，为吾有身也。及吾无身，有何梡（患）？故贵为身于为天下，若可以迈（托）天下矣；爱以身为天下，女何〈可〉以寄天下。视之而弗见，名之曰微。听之而弗闻，名之曰希。揞之而弗得，名之曰夷。三者不可至（致）计（诘），故園【而为一】。一者，其上不攸，其下不忽。寻寻呵不可名也，复归于无物。是胃（谓）无状之状，无物之【象。是谓忽恍。随而不见其后，迎】而不见其首。执今之道，以御今之有，以知古始，是胃（谓）【道纪。古之善为道者，微妙玄达】，深不可志（识）。夫唯不可志（识），故强为之容，曰：与呵其若冬【涉水，犹呵其若】畏四【邻，严】呵其若客，涣呵其若淩（凌）泽（释），□呵其若楃（朴），湷【呵其若浊，湛呵其】若浴（谷）。浊而情（静）之，余（徐）清。女〈安〉以重（动）之，余（徐）生。葆此道不欲盈。夫唯不欲【盈，是】以能【敝而不】成。至虚极也，守情（静）表也。万物旁（并）作，吾以观其复也。天物云云，各复归于其【根，曰静。】情（静），是胃（谓）复命。复命，常也。知常，明也。不知常，帍（妄），帍（妄）作凶。知常容，容乃公，公乃王，王乃天，天乃道，【道乃久】，沕（没）身不怠。大上下知有之，其次亲誉之，其次畏之，其下母（侮）之。信不足，案有不信。【犹呵】其贵言也。成功遂事，而百省（姓）胃（谓）我自然。故大道广，案有仁义。知（智）快（慧）出，案有大伪。六亲不和，案有畜（孝）兹（慈）。邦家闆（昏）乱，案有贞臣。绝声（圣）弃知（智），民利百负（倍）。绝仁弃义，民复畜（孝）兹（慈）。绝巧弃利，盗贼无有。此三言也，以为文未足，故令之有所属。见素抱【朴，少私寡欲。绝学无忧】。唯与诃，其相去几何？美与恶，其相去何若？人之【所畏】，亦不【可以不畏。恍呵其未央哉】！·众人巸（熙）巸（熙），若乡（飨）于大牢，而春登台。我泊焉未佻（兆），若【婴儿未咳】。累呵如【无所归。众人】皆有余，我独遗。我禺（愚）人之心也，惷惷呵。鬻（俗）【人昭昭，我独若】闆（昏）呵。鬻（俗）人蔡（察）蔡（察），我独闆（闷）闆（闷）呵。忽呵其若【海】，望（恍）呵其若无所止。【众人皆有以，我独顽】以悝（俚）。吾欲独异于人，而贵食母。孔德之容，唯道是从。道之物，唯望（恍）唯忽。【忽呵恍】呵，中有象呵。望（恍）呵忽呵，中有物呵。滣（幽）呵鸣（冥）呵，中有请（精）吔（呵）。其请（精）甚真，其中【有信】。自今及古，其名不去，以顺众仪（父）。吾何以知众仪（父）之然？以此。炊者不立，自视（示）不章，【自】见者不明，自伐者无功，自矜者不长。其在道，曰："粽（余）食、赘行。"物或恶之，故有欲者【弗】居。曲则金（全），枉则定（正），洼则盈，敝则新。少则得，多则惑。是以声（圣）人执一，以为天下牧。不【自】视（示）故明，不自见故章，不自伐故有功，弗矜故能长。夫唯不争，故莫能与之争。古【之所谓曲全者几】语才（哉），诚金（全）归之。希言自然。飘风不冬（终）朝，暴雨不冬（终）日。孰为此？天地，【而弗能久，又况】于【人乎】？故从事而道者同于道，德（得）者同于德（得），者〈失〉者同于失。同德（得）【者】，道亦德（得）之。同于失者，道亦失之。有物昆成，先天地生。绣（寂）呵缪（寥）呵，独立【而不改】，可以为天地母。吾未知其名，字之曰道。吾强为之名曰大。【大】曰筮（逝），筮（逝）曰【远，远曰反。道大】，天大，地大，王亦大。国中有四大，而王居一焉。人法地，【地】法【天】，天法【道，道】法【自然。重】为坙（轻）根，清（静）为趮（躁）君。是以君子众（终）日行，不离其甾（辎）重，唯（虽）有环官，燕处【则昭】若。若何万乘之王而以身坙（轻）于天下？坙（轻）则失本，趮（躁）则失君。善行者无勶（辙）迹，【善】言者无瑕適（谪），善数者不以梼（筹）箖（策）。善闭者无閪（关）籥（闔）而不可启也，善结者【无纆】约而不可解也。是以声（圣）人恒善怵（救）人，而无弃人，物无弃财，是胃（谓）愧明。故善【人，善人】之师；不善人，善人之齎（资）也。不贵其师，不爱其齎（资），唯（虽）知（智）乎大眯（迷）。是胃（谓）眇（妙）要。知其雄，守其雌，为天下溪。为天下溪，恒德不鸡〈离〉。恒〈德〉不鸡〈离〉，复归婴儿。知其白，守其辱，为天下。为天下浴（谷），恒德乃【足】。德乃【足，复归于朴】。知其，守其黑，为天下式。为天下式，恒德不貣（忒）。德不貣（忒），复归于无极。楃（朴）散【则为器，圣】人用则为官长。夫大制无割。将欲取天下而为之，吾见其弗【得已。夫天下，神】器也，非可为者也。为者败之，执者失之。物或行或随，或炅（热）或【吹，或强或挫】，或坏（培）或撱（堕）。是以声（圣）人去甚，去大，去楮（奢）。以道佐人主，不以兵强【于】天下。【其事好还，师之】所居，楚朸（棘）生之。善者果而已矣，毋以取强焉。果而毋驕（骄），果而勿矜，果而【勿伐】，果而毋得已居，是胃（谓）【果】而不强。物壮而老，是胃（谓）之不道，不道蚤（早）已。夫兵者，不祥之器【也】。物或恶之，故有欲者弗居。君子居则贵左，用兵则贵右。故兵者非君子之器也。【兵者】不祥之器也，不得已而用之，铦袭为上，勿美也。若美之，是乐杀人也。夫乐杀人，不可以得志于天下矣。是以吉事上左，丧事上右；是以便（偏）将军居左，上将军居右，言以丧礼居之也。

杀人众,以悲依(哀)立(莅)之;战胜,以丧礼处之。道恒无名,楃(朴)唯(虽)【小而天下弗敢臣。侯】王若能守之,万物将自宾。天地相谷〈合〉,以俞甘洛(露)。民莫之【令,而自】均焉。始制有【名。名亦既】有,夫【亦将知止,知止】所以不【殆】。俾(譬)道之在天【下也,犹小】浴(谷)之与江海也。知人者,知(智)也。自知【者,明也。胜人】者,有力也。自胜者,【强也。知足者,富】也。强行者,有志也。不失其所者,久也。死不忘者,寿也。道泛【呵其可左右也,成功】遂事而弗名有也。万物归焉而弗为主,则恒无欲也,可名于小。万物归焉【而弗】为主,可名于大。是【以】声(圣)人之能成大也,以其不为大也,故能成大。执大象,【天下】往。往而不害,安平大。乐与饵,过格(客)止。故道之出言也,曰:"谈(淡)呵其无味也。【视之】,不足见也。听之,不足闻也。用之,不可既也。"将欲拾(翕)之,必古(固)张之。将欲弱之,【必固】强之。将欲去之,必古(固)与之。将欲夺之,必古(固)予之。是胃(谓)微明。友弱胜强,鱼不脱于潚(渊),邦利器不可以视(示)人。道恒无名,侯王若守之,万物将自憃(化)。憃(化)而欲【作,吾将镇之以无】名之楃(朴)。【镇之以】无名之楃(朴),夫将不辱。不辱以情(静),天地将自正。

马王堆汉墓帛书《德道经》乙本

德　经

上德不德,是以有德。下德不失德,是以无德。上德无为而无以为也。上仁为之而无以为也。上德〈义〉为之而有以为也。上礼为之而莫之应也,则攘臂而乃(扔)之。故失道而后德,失德而句(后)仁,失仁而句(后)义,失义而句(后)礼。夫礼者,忠信之泊(薄)也,而乱之首也。前识者,道之华也,而愚之首也。是以大丈夫居【其厚不】居其泊(薄),居其实而不居其华。故去罢(彼)而取此。昔得一者,天得一以清,地得一以宁,神得一以霝(灵),浴(谷)得一盈,侯王得一以为天下正。其至也,胃(谓)天毋已清将恐莲(裂),地毋已宁将恐发,神毋【已灵将】恐歇,谷毋已【盈】将渴(竭),侯王毋已贵以高将欮(蹶)。故必贵以贱为本,必高矣而以下为基。夫是以侯王自胃(谓)孤寡不橐(縠),此其贱之本与?非也?故至数舆无舆。是故不欲禄禄若玉,硌硌若石。上【士闻】道,堇(勤)能行之。中士闻道,若存若亡。下士闻道,大笑之。弗笑【不足】以为道。是以建言有之曰:明道如费,进道如退,夷道如类。上德如浴(谷),大白如辱,广德如不足。建德如【偷】,质【真如渝】,大方无禺(隅),大器免(晚)成,大音希声,天〈大〉象无刑(形),道褒无名。夫唯道,善始且善成。反也者,道之动也。【弱也】者,道之用也。天下之物生于有,有【生】于无。道生一,一生二,二生三,三生【万物。万物负阴而抱阳,中气】以为和。人之所亚(恶),唯孤寡不橐(縠),而王公以自【称也。物或益之而】云(损),云(损)之而益。【人之所教,亦议而教人。强梁者不得其死】,吾将以【为学】父。天下之至【柔】,驰骋乎天下【之至坚。出于无有,入于】无间。吾是以【知无为之有益】也。不【言之教,无为之益,天下希能及之】矣。名与【身孰亲?身与货孰多?得与亡孰病?甚爱必大费,多藏必厚亡。故知足不辱,知止不殆,可以长久。大成如缺,其用不敝。大】盈如冲,其【用不穷。大直如诎,大辩如讷,大】巧如拙,【大赢如】绌。趮(躁)朕(胜)寒,【静胜热。知清静,可以为天下正。天下有】道,却走马【以】粪。无道,戎马生于郊。罪莫大可欲,祸【莫大于不知足,咎莫憯于欲得。故知足之足,恒】足矣。不出于户,以知天下。不规(窥)于【牖,以】知天道。其出祭(弥)远者,其知祭(弥)【鲜。是以圣人不行而知,不见】而名,弗为而成。为学者日益,闻道者日云(损),云(损)之有

(又)云(损),以至于无【为,无为而无不为矣。将欲】取天下,恒无事,及其有事也,【又不】足以取天【下矣。圣】人恒无心,以百省(姓)之心为心。善【者善之,不善者亦善之,得】善也。信者信之,不信者亦信之,德(得)信也。耶(圣)人之在天下也欲(歙)欲(歙)焉,【为天下浑心,百】生(姓)皆注其【耳目焉,圣人皆咳之。出】生,入死。生之【徒十有三,死】之徒十又(有)三,而民生生,僮(动)皆之死地之十有三。【夫】何故也?以其生生。盖闻善执生者,陵行不辟(避)兕虎,入军不被兵革。兕无【所椯其角,虎无所措】其蚤(爪),兵【无所容其刃,夫何故】也?以其无【死地焉】。道生之,德畜之,物刑(形)之而器成之。是以万物尊道而贵德。道之尊也,德之贵也,夫莫之爵也,而恒自然也。道生之,畜【之,长之,育】之,亭之,毒之,养之,复(覆)【之。生而弗有,为而弗恃,长而】弗宰,是胃(谓)玄德。天下有始,以为天下母。既得其母,以知其子,既○知其子,复守其母,没身不佁(殆)。塞其垸,闭其门,冬(终)身不堇(勤)。启其垸,齐其【事,终身】不棘。见小曰明,守【柔曰】强。用【其光,复归其明。无】遗身央(殃),是胃(谓)【袭】常。使我介有知,行于大道,唯他(施)是畏。大道甚夷,民甚好解。朝甚除,田甚芜,仓甚虚;服文采,带利剑,猒(厌)食而赍(资)财【有余,是谓】盗□。【盗】□,非【道】也。善建者【不拔,善抱者不脱】,子孙以祭祀不绝。脩之身,其德乃真。脩之家,其德有余。脩之乡,其德乃长。脩之国,其德乃夆(丰)。脩之天下,其德乃博(溥)。以身观身,以家观【家,以国观】国,以天下观天下。吾何【以】知天下之然兹(哉)?以【此】。含德之厚者,比于赤子。螽(蜂)疠(虿)虫(虺)蛇弗赫(螫),据鸟孟(猛)兽弗捕(搏),骨筋弱柔而握固。未知牝牡之会而朘怒,精之至也。冬(终)日号而不嚘,和【之至也。知和曰】常,知常曰明,益生【曰】祥,心使气曰强。物【壮】则老,胃(谓)之不道,不道蚤(早)已。知者弗言,言者弗知。塞其埦,闭其门,和其光,同其尘,锉(挫)其兑(锐)而解其纷,是胃(谓)玄同。故不可得而亲也,亦【不可】得而【疏;不可】得而○利,【亦不可】得而害;不可得而贵,亦不可得而贱。故为天下贵。以正之(治)国,以畸(奇)用兵,以无事取天下。吾何以知其然也才(哉)?夫天下多忌讳,而民弥贫。民多利器,【而国家滋】昏。【人多智慧,而奇物滋起。法】物兹(滋)章,而盗贼【多有】。是以【圣】人之言曰:我无为而民自化,我好静而民自正,我无事而民自富,我欲不欲而民自朴。其正(政)闅(闵)闅(闵),其民屯屯。其正(政)察察,其【民缺缺】。福,【祸】之所伏,孰知其极?【其】无正也?正【复为奇】,善复为【妖。人】之悉(迷)也,其日固久矣。是以方而不割,兼(廉)而不刺,直而不绁,光而不眺(耀)。治人事天,莫若啬。夫唯啬,是以蚤(早)服。蚤(早)服是胃(谓)重积【德】。重【积德则无不克,无不克则】莫知其【极】。莫知其【极,可以】有国。有国之母,可【以长】久。是胃(谓)【深】根固氐(柢),长生久视之道也。治大国若亨(烹)小鲜。以道立(莅)天下,其鬼不神。非其鬼不神也,其神不伤人也。非其神不伤人也,【圣人亦】弗伤也。夫两【不】相伤,故德交归焉。大国【者,下流也,天下之】牝也。天下之交也,牝恒以静朕(胜)牡。为其静也,故宜为下也㉖。故大国以下【小】国,则取小国。小国以下大国,则取于大国。故或下【以取,或】下而取。故大国者不【过】欲并畜人,小国不【过】欲入事人。夫【皆得】其欲,则大者宜为下。道者,万物之注也,善人之琛(宝)也,不善人之所保也。美言可以市,尊行可以贺(加)人。人之不善,何【弃之有?故】立天子,置三乡〈卿〉,虽有【共之】璧以先四马,不若坐而进此。古【之所以贵此道者何也】?不胃(谓)求以得,有罪以免与?故为天下贵。为无为,【事无事,味无味。大小多少,报怨以德。图难乎其易也,为大】乎其细也。天下之【难作于】易,天下之大【作于细。是以圣人终不为大,故能成其大】。夫轻若(诺)【必寡】信,多易必多难,是以耶(圣)人【犹难】之,故【终于无难。其安也易持,其未兆也易谋,其脆也易判,其微也易散。为之于其未有也,治之于其未乱也。合抱之】木,作于毫末。九成之台,作于蘽(蔂)土。百千之高,始于足下。为之者败之,执者失之。是以耶(圣)人无为【也,故无败也;无执也,故无失也】。民之从事也,恒于其成而败之。故曰:“慎冬(终)若始,则无败事矣。”是以耶(圣)人欲不欲,而不贵难得之货;学不学,复众人之所过;能辅万物之自然,而弗敢为。古之为道者,非以明【民也,将以愚】之也。夫民之难治也,以其知(智)也。故以知(智)知国,国之贼也;以不知(智)知国,国之德也;恒知此两者,亦稽式也。恒知稽式,是胃(谓)玄德。玄德深矣、远矣,【与】物反也,乃至大顺。江海所以能为百浴(谷)【王者,以】其【善】下之也,是以能为百浴(谷)王。是以耶(圣)人之欲上民也,必以其言下之;其欲先民也,必以其身后之。故居上而民弗重也,居前而民弗害。天下皆乐谁(推)而弗猒(厌)也,不【以】其无争与?故天下莫能与争。小国寡民,使有十百人器而勿用,使民重死而远徙。又(有)周(舟)车无所乘之,有甲兵无所陈之。使民复结绳而用之。甘其食,美其服,乐其俗,安其居。哭(邻)国相望,鸡犬之【声相】闻,民至老死不相往来。信言不美,美言不信。知者不博,博者不知。善者不多,多者不善。耶(圣)人无积,既以为人,己俞(愈)有;既以予人矣,己俞(愈)多。故天之道,利而不害;人之道,为而弗争。天下【皆】胃(谓)我大,大而不宵(肖)。夫唯不宵(肖),故能大。若宵(肖),久矣其细也夫。我恒有三琛(宝),市(持)而琛(宝)之,一曰兹(慈),二曰检(俭),三曰不敢为天下先。夫兹(慈),故能勇;检(俭),敢〈故〉能广;不敢为天下先,故能为成器长。今舍其兹(慈),且勇;舍其检

(俭),且广;舍其后,且先;则死矣。夫兹(慈),以单(战)则朕(胜),以守则固。天将建之,如以兹(慈)垣之。故善为士者不武,善单(战)者不怒,善朕(胜)敌者弗与,善用人者为之下。是胃(谓)不争【之】德。是胃(谓)用人,是胃(谓)肥(配)天,古之极也。用兵又(有)言曰:吾不敢为主而为客,不敢进寸而退尺。是胃(谓)行无行,攘无臂,执无兵,乃(扔)无敌。祸莫大于无敌。无敌近〇亡吾琛(宝)矣。故抗兵相若,而依(哀)者朕(胜)【矣】。吾言易知也,易行也;而天下莫之能知也,莫之能行也。夫言又(有)宗,事又(有)君。夫唯无知也,是以不我知。知者希,则我贵矣。是以耶(圣)人被褐而褱(怀)玉。知不知,尚矣;不知知,病矣。是以耶(圣)人之不【病】也,以其病病也,是以不病,民之不畏畏(威),则大畏(威)将至矣。毋伊(狎)其所居,毋猒(厌)其所生。夫唯弗猒(厌),是以不猒(厌)。是以耶(圣)人自知而不自见也,自爱而不自贵也。故去罢(彼)而取此。勇于敢则杀,勇于不敢则栝(活),【此】两者或利或害。天之所亚(恶),熟知其故?天之道,不单(战)而善朕(胜),不言而善应,弗召而自来,单(坦)而善谋。天罔(网)袶袶,疏而不失。若民恒且〇不畏死,若何以杀曜(惧)之也?使民恒且畏死,而为畸(奇)者【吾】得而杀之,夫孰敢矣!若民恒且必畏死,则恒又(有)司杀者。夫代司杀者杀,是代大匠斫。夫代大匠斫,则希不伤其手。人之饥也,以其取食跷之多,是以饥。百生(姓)之不治也,以其上之有以为也,【是】以不治。民之轻死也,以其求生之厚也,是以轻死。夫唯无以生为者,是贤贵生。人之生也柔弱,其死也髄信坚强。万【物草】木之生也柔椊(脆),其死也椩(枯)槁。故曰:“坚强,死之徒也;柔弱,生之徒也”。【是】以兵强则不朕(胜),木强则兢。故强大居下,柔弱居上。天之道,酉(犹)张弓也,高者印(抑)之,下者举之,有余(馀)者云(损)之,不足者【补之。故天下之道】,

云(损)有余(馀)而益不足;人之道,云(损)不足而奉又(有)余(馀)。夫孰能又(有)余(馀)而【有以】奉于天者,唯又(有)道者乎?是以耶(圣)人为而弗又(有),成功而弗居也。若此其不欲见贤也。天下莫柔弱于水,【而攻坚强者莫之能先】,以其无以易之也。水之朕(胜)刚也,弱之朕(胜)强也,天下莫弗知也,而【莫之能行】也。是故耶(圣)人之言云,曰:受国之訽(诟),是胃(谓)社稷之主。受国之不祥,是胃(谓)天下之王。正言若反。禾(和)大【怨,必有余怨,安可以】为善?是以耶(圣)人执左芥(契)而不以责于人。故又(有)德司芥(契),无德司勶(彻)。【天道无亲,常与善人】。《德》三千册一。

道 经

道,可道也,【非恒道也。名,可名也,非】恒名也。无名,万物之始也。有名,万物之母也。故恒无欲也,【以观其妙】;恒又(有)欲也,以观其所噭。两者同出,异名同胃(谓)。玄之又玄,众眇(妙)之门。天下皆知美之为美,亚(恶)已。皆知善,斯不善矣。【有、无之相】生也,难、易之相成也,长、短之相刑(形)也,高、下之相盈也,音、声之相和也,先、后之相隋(随),恒也。是以耶(圣)人居无为之事,行不言之教。万物昔(作)而弗始[1],为而弗侍(恃)也,成功而弗居也。夫唯弗居,是以弗去。不上贤,使民不争。不贵难得之货,使民不为盗。不见可欲,使民不乱。是以耶(圣)人之治也,虚其心,实其腹;弱其志,强其骨。恒使民无知无欲也。使夫知不敢弗为而已,则无不治矣。道冲,而用之有(又)弗盈也。渊呵佁(似)万物之宗。锉(挫)其兑(锐),解其芬(纷);和其光,同其尘。湛呵佁(似)或存。吾不知其谁之子也,象帝之先。天地不仁,以万物为刍狗。耶(圣)人不仁,【以】百姓为刍狗。天地之间,其猷(犹)橐籥舆(与)?虚而不淈(屈),动而俞(愈)出。多闻数穷,不若守于中。浴(谷)神不死,是胃

（谓）玄牝。玄牝之门，是胃（谓）天地之根。绵绵呵其若存，用之不堇（勤）。天长，地久。天地之所以能长且久者，以其不自生也，故能长生。是以耶（圣）人退其身而身先，外其身而身先，外其身而身存。不以其无私舆（与）？故能成其私。上善如水。水善利万物而有争，居众人之所亚（恶），故几于道矣。居善地，心善渊，予善天，言善信，正（政）善治，事善能，动善时。夫唯不争，故无尤。揗（持）而盈之，不若其已。㧑（揣）而允之，不可长葆也。金玉盈室，莫之能守也。贵富而骄，自遗咎也。功遂身退，天之道也。戴营袙（魄）抱一，能毋离乎？槫（抟）气至柔，能婴儿乎？脩（涤）除玄监（鉴），能毋有疵乎？爱民栝（活）国，能毋以知乎？天门启阖，能为雌乎？明白四达，能毋以知乎？生之，畜之，生而弗有，长而弗宰也，是胃（谓）玄德。卅楅（辐）同一毂，当其无有，车之用也。燃（埏）埴而为器，当其无有，埴器之用也。鑿户牖，当其无有，室之用也。故有之以为利，无之以为用。五色使人目盲，驰骋田腊（猎）使人心发狂，难得之货〇使人之行仿（妨）。五味使人之口爽，五音使人之耳（聋）。是以耶（圣）人之治也，为腹而不为目。故去彼而取此。弄（宠）辱若惊，贵大患若身。何胃（谓）弄（宠）辱若惊？弄（宠）之为下也，得之若惊，失之若惊，是胃（谓）弄（宠）辱若惊。何胃（谓）贵大患若身？吾所以有大患者，为吾有身也。及吾无身，有何患？故贵为身于为天下，若可以橐（托）天下【矣】；爱以身为天下，女可以寄天下矣。视之而弗见，【名】之曰微。听之而弗闻，命（名）之曰希。〇揺之而弗得，命（名）之曰夷。三者不可至（致）计（诘），故绢而为一。一者，其上不谬，其下不忽。寻寻呵不可命（名）也，复归于无物。是胃（谓）无状之状，无物之象。是胃（谓）沕（忽）望（恍）。隋（随）而不见其后，迎而不见其首。执今之道，以御今之有。以知古始，是胃（谓）道纪。古之□为道者，微眇（妙）玄达，深不可志（识）。

夫唯不可志(识),故强为之容,曰:与呵其若冬涉水,猷(犹)呵其若畏四哭(鄰),严呵其若客,涣呵其若淩(凌)泽(释),沌呵其若朴,湷呵其若浊,湛呵其若浴(谷)。浊而静之,徐清。女〈安〉以重(动)之,徐生。葆此道【者不】欲盈。是以能㢸(敝)而不成。至虚极也,守静督也。万物旁(并)作,吾以观其复也。天物祛(魂)祛(魂),各复归于其根。曰静。静,是胃(谓)复命。复命,常也。知常,明也。不知常,芒(妄),芒(妄)作凶。知常容,容乃公,公乃王,【王乃】天,天乃道,道乃。没身不殆。大上下知又(有)【之】,其【次】亲誉之,其次畏之,其下母(侮)之。信不足,安有不信。猷(犹)呵其贵言也。成功遂事,而百姓胃(谓)我自然。故大道废,安有仁义。知(智)慧出,安有【大伪】。六亲不和,安又(有)孝兹(慈)。国家闅(昏)乱,安有贞臣。绝耶(圣)弃知(智),而民利百倍。绝仁弃义,而民复孝兹(慈)。绝巧弃利,盗贼无有。此三言也,以为文未足,故令之有所属。见素抱朴,少私而寡欲。绝学无忧。唯与呵,其相去几何?美与亚(恶),其相去何若?人之所畏,亦不可以不畏人。望(恍)呵其未央才(哉)!众人配(熙)配(熙),若乡(飨)于大牢,而春登台。我博(泊)焉未垗(兆),若婴儿未咳。累呵佁(似)无所归。众人皆又(有)余(馀)。我愚人之心也,湷湷呵。鬻(俗)人昭昭,我独若闅(昏)呵。鬻(俗)人察察,我独闽(闵)闽(闵)呵。沕(忽)呵其若海,望(恍)呵若无所止。众人皆有以,我独门元(顽)以鄙。吾欲独异于人,而贵食母。孔德之容,唯道是从。道之物,唯望(恍)唯沕(忽)。沕(忽)呵望(恍)呵,中又(有)象呵。望(恍)呵沕(忽)呵,中有物呵。幼(窈)呵冥呵,其中有请(精)呵。其请(精)甚真,其中有信。自今及古,其名不去,以顺众父。吾何以知众父之然也?以此。炊者不立。自视(示)者不章,自见者不明,自伐者无功,自矜者不长。其在道也,曰:"粽(馀)食、赘行。"物或亚(恶)之,故有欲者弗居。曲则全,汪(枉)则正,洼则盈,褩(敝)则新。少则得,多则惑。是以耶(圣)人执一,以为天下牧。不自视(示)故章,不自见也故明,不自伐故有功,弗矜故能长。夫唯不争,故莫能与之争。古之所胃(谓)曲全者几语才(哉),诚全归之。希言自然。薊(飘)风不冬(终)朝,暴雨不冬(终)日。孰为此?天地,而弗能久,有(又)兄(况)于人乎?故从事而道者同于道,德(得)者同于德(得),失者同于失。同于德(得)者,道亦德(得)之;同于失者,道亦失之。有物昆成,先天地生。萧(寂)呵漻(寥)呵,独立而不玹(改),可以为天地母。吾未知其名也,字之曰道。吾强为之名曰大。大曰筮(逝),筮(逝)曰远,远曰反。道大,天大,地大,王亦大。国中有四大,而王居一焉。人法地,地法天,天法道,道法自然。重为轻根,静为趮(躁)君。是以君子冬(终)日行,不远其甾(辎)重,虽有环官(馆),燕处则昭若。若何万乘之王而以身轻于天下?轻则失本,趮(躁)则失君。善行者无达迹,善言者无瑕適(谪),善数者不用梼(筹)箖(策)。善○闭者无关籥(闗)而不可启也,善结者无纆约而不可解也。是以耶(圣)人恒善怺(救)人,而无弃人,物无弃财,是胃(谓)曳(愧)明。故善人,善人之师;不善人,善人之资也。不贵其师,不爱其资,虽知(智)乎大迷。是胃(谓)眇(妙)要。知其雄,守其雌,为天下鸡(溪)。为天下鸡(溪),恒德不离。恒德不离,复【归于婴儿。知】其白,守其辱,为天下○浴(谷)。为天下浴(谷),恒德乃足。恒德乃足,复归于朴。知其白,守其黑,为天下式。为天下式,恒德不贷(忒)。恒德不贷(忒),复归于无极。朴散则为器,耶(圣)人用则为官长。夫大制无割。将欲取【天下而为之,吾见其弗】得已。夫天下,神器也,非可为者也。为之者败之,执之者失之。○物或行或隋(随),或热,或碰,或陪(培)或堕。是以耶(圣)人去甚,去大,去诸(奢)。以道佐人主,不以兵强于天下。其

【事好还，师之所处，荆】棘生之。善者果而已矣，毋以取强焉。果而毋骄，果而勿矜，果【而毋】伐，果而毋得已居，是胃(谓)果而强。物壮而老，胃(谓)之不道，不道蚤(早)已。夫兵者，不祥之器也。物或亚(恶)【之，故有欲者弗居。君】子居则贵左，用兵则贵右。故兵者非君子之器。兵者不祥【之】器也，不得已而用之，铦憹为上，勿美也。若美之，是乐杀人也。夫乐杀人，不可以得志于天下矣。是以吉事【上左，丧事上右】；是以偏将军居左，而上将军居右，言以丧礼居之也。杀【人众，以悲哀】立(莅)【之；战】朕(胜)而以丧礼处之。道恒无名，朴唯(虽)小而天下弗敢臣。侯王若能守之，万物将自宾。天地相合，以俞甘洛(露)。【民莫之】令，而自均焉。始制有名，名亦既有，夫亦将知止，知止所以不殆。卑(譬)【道之】在天下也，猷(犹)小浴(谷)之与江海也。知人者，知(智)也。自知，明也。朕(胜)人者，有力也。自朕(胜)者，强也。知足者，富也。强行者，有志也。不失其所者，久也。死而不忘者，寿也。道，沨(泛)呵其可左右也，成功遂【事而】弗名有也。万物归焉而弗为主，则恒无欲也，可名于小。万物归焉而弗为主，可命(名)于大。是以耶(圣)人之能成大也，以其不为大也，故能成大。执大象，天下往。往而不害，安平大。乐与【饵】，过格(客)止。故道之出言也，曰："淡呵其无味也。视之，不足见也。听之，不足闻也。用之不可既也"。将欲擒(翕)之，必古(固)张之。将欲弱之，必古(固)○强之。将欲去之，必古(固)与之。将欲夺之，必古(固)予【之】。是胃(谓)微明。柔弱朕(胜)强。鱼不可说(脱)于渊，国利器不可以示人。道恒无名，侯王若能守之，万物将自化。化而欲作，吾将阗(镇)之以无名之朴。阗(镇)之以无名之朴，夫将不辱。不辱以静，天地将自正。

《道》二千四百廿六

索引 Index

本索引的原则是：凡书中所出现的重要概念一概收入，每个概念下详列实例。按汉语拼音字母顺序排列。每例后均在括号里注明章号和页码。如：道可道非常道 the Way that can be told of is not an Unvarying Way(1.1)。圆点前的数字为章号，之后的数字为页码。

夫兵者不祥之器	fine weapons are none the less ill-omened things(31.66)
用兵则贵右	in war the right-hand side is the place of honour(31.66)
兵者不祥之器	weapons are ill-omened things(31.66)
入军不被甲兵	in battle he is not touched by weapons of war(50.110)
兵无所容其刃	a weapon would find no place for its point to enter in (50.110)
以奇用兵	battles can only be won if rules are broken(57.125)
用兵有言	the strategists have the sayings(69.153)
执无兵	a host that can confront, yet presents no battle-front(69.153)
故抗兵相若	when armies are raised and issues joined (69.153)
兵强则灭	the hard and mighty are cast down(76.167)
虽有甲兵无所陈之	there might still be weapons of war but no one would drill with them(80.175)

C

长

长短相形	long and short test one another(2.3)
天长地久	Heaven is Eternal, the Earth everlasting (7.13)
天地所以能长且久者	how come they to be so(7.13)

以其不自生故能长生	they do not foster their own lives; that is why they live so long(7.13)
不可长保	you will find it soon grows dull(9.17)
不自矜故长	he is not proud of his work, and therefore it endures(22.45)
自矜者不长	he who is proud of his work, achieves nothing that endures(24.49)
知止不殆可以长久	stops in time nothing can harm he is forever safe and secure(44.98)
修之于乡其德乃长	apply it to the village, and the village will be made secure(54.118)
有国之母可以长久	he who having the kingdom goes to the Mother can keep it long(59.129)
长生久视之道	making life long by fixed staring(59.129)

常

道可道非常道	the Way that can be told of is not an Unvarying Way(1.1)
名可名非常名	the names that can be named are not unvarying names (1.1)
故常无欲以观其妙	only he that rids himself forever of desire can see the Secret Essences(1.1)
常有欲以观其徼	he that has never rid himself of desire can see only the Outcomes(1.1)
常使民无知无欲	ever striving to make the people knowledgeless and desireless(3.5)
复命曰常	what has submitted to Fate has become part of the always-so (16.32)
知常曰明	to know the always-so is to be illumined

male(61.133)

常于几成而败之	constantly spoil things when within an ace of completing them(64.141)
常知稽式	to be always able to apply this test and standard(65.144)
若使民常畏死	even supposing people were generally frightened of death (74.163)
常有司杀者杀	there is the Lord of Slaughter always ready for this task (74.163)
天道无亲常与善人	it is Heaven's way, without distinction of persons, to keep the good perpetually supplied(79.173)

常德

常德不离	he knows all the time a power that he never calls upon in vain(28.59)
常德不忒	he has all the time a power that never errs (28.59)
常德乃足	he has all the time a power that suffices (28.59)

成

难易相成	difficult and easy complete one another (2.3)
功成而弗居	achieves his aim, but does not call attention to what he does(2.3)
故能成其私	that all his personal ends are fulfilled(7.13)
故能敝而新成	they are like a garment that endures all

D

大

贵大患若身	high rank hurts keenly as our bodies hurt (13.25)
何谓贵大患若身	what does it mean to say that high rank hurts keenly as our bodies hurt(13.25)
吾所以有大患者	the only reason that we suffer hurt(13.25)
大道废	it was when the Great Way declined(18.36)
有大伪	the Great Artifice began(18.36)
强为之名曰大	were I forced to say to what class of things it belongs I should called it Great (25.51)
大曰逝	now ta also means passing on(25.51)
故道大	as Tao has this greatness(25.51)
天大	as heaven has it(25.51)
地大	as earth has it(25.51)
人亦大	so may the ruler also have it (so may man have it) (25.51)
域中有四大	within the realm there are four portions of greatness(25.51)
虽智大迷	much learning though he may possess, is far astray(27.56)
故大制不割	the greatest carver does the least cutting (28.59)
大军之后	the raising of a great host(30.64)
大道泛兮	Great Tao is like a boat that drifts(34.72)

	others want(46.102)
祸莫大于不知足	no disaster greater than not to be content with what one has(46.102)
行于大道	got started on the great highway(53.116)
大道甚夷	great highways are safe and easy (53.116)
治大国	ruling a large kingdom(60.131)
大邦者下流	a large kingdom must be like the low ground towards which all streams flow down(61.133)
故大邦以下小邦	a large kingdom can in the same way succeed in getting underneath a small kingdom(61.133)
小邦以下大邦	small kingdoms are by nature in this way underneath large kingdoms(61.133)
则取于大邦	they win the adherence of large kingdoms (61.133)
大邦不过欲兼畜人	what large countries really need is more inhabitants (the large nation wants nothing more than to ally and nurture the people) (61.133)
大者宜为下	the large kingdom must "get underneath" (61.133)
大小多少	make the small great and the few many (63.139)
为大于其细	deals with the great while it is still small (63.139)
天下大事	in the governance of empire(63.139)

	varying Way (1.1)
道冲	the Way is like an empty vessel (4.7)
故几于道	that makes water so near to the Way (8.15)
天之道也	such is Heaven's Way (9.17)
执古之道	by seizing on the Way that was (14.27)
是谓道纪	this is called the essence of the Way (14.27)
保此道者	those who possess this Tao (15.29)
天乃道	to be of heaven is to be in Tao (16.32)
道乃久	Tao is forever (16.32)
大道废	it was when the Great Way declined (18.36)
惟道是从	it alone can act through the Way (21.43)
道之为物惟恍惟惚	the Way is a thing impalpable, incommensurable(21.43)
故从事于道者同于道	if one uses the Way as one's instrument, the results will be like the Way (23.47)
同于道者道亦乐得之	to those who have conformed themselves to the Way, the Way readily lends it power (23.47)
其在道也	from the standpoint of the Way (24.49)
故有道者不处	that is why he that possesses Tao does not linger (24.49)
强字之曰道	"Way" is the by-name that we give it (25.51)
故道大	Tao has "this greatness"(25.51)
天法道	the ways of heaven (are conditioned) by

	Tao (41.90)
下士闻道	when the man of low capacity hears Tao (41.90)
不笑不足以为道	if he did not laugh, it would not be worth the name of Tao (41.90)
明道若昧	the way out into the light often looks dark (41.90)
进道若退	the way that goes ahead often looks as if it went back (41.90)
夷道若纇	the way that is least hilly often looks as if it went up and down (41.90)
道隐无名	Tao is hidden and nameless (41.90)
夫唯道善贷且成	Tao alone supports all things and brings them to fulfilment (41.90)
道生一	Tao gave birth to the One (42.93)
天下有道	when there is Tao in the empire (46.102)
天下无道	when there is not Tao in the empire (46.102)
见天道	he knows all the ways of heaven (47.104)
为道日损	the practice of Tao consists in substracting day by day (48.106)
道生之	Tao gave them birth (51.112)
尊道	worship Tao (51.112)
道之尊	Tao the right to be worshipped (51.112)
故道生之	as Tao bore them (51.112)
行于大道	he has got started on the great highway (53.116)

人之道	the Sage's way (81.177)

德

是谓玄德	this is called the Mysterious Power (10.19)
孔德之容	such the scope of the All-pervading Power (21.43)
德者同于德	if one uses the "power" as one's instrument, the results will be like the "power" (23.47)
同于德者德亦乐得之	to those who have conformed themselves to the power, the power readily, lends more power (23.47)
常德不离	a power that he never calls upon in vain (28.59)
常德不忒	he has all the time a power that never errs (28.59)
常德乃足	he has all the time a power that suffices (28.59)
上德不德是以有德	the man of highest "power" does not reveal himself as a possessor of "power"; therefore he keeps his "power" (38.80)
下德不失德是以无德	the man of inferior "power" cannot rid it of the appearance of "power"; therefore he is in truth without "power" (38.80)
上德无为	the man of highest "power" neither acts (38.80)
下德无为而有以为	the man of inferior "power" both acts and is so regarded (38.80)
故失道而后德	after Tao was lost, then came the "power"

	tended(54.118)
含德之厚	the impunity of things fraught with the "power"(55.120)
早服谓之重积德	"quickly absorbing" means doubling one's garnered "power"(59.129)
重积德	double your garnered power(59.129)
故德交归焉	their "power" could converge towards a common end(60.131)
报怨以德	requites injuries with good deeds (63.131)
是谓玄德	is called the mysterious "power" (65.144)
玄德深矣	the mysterious "power," so deep-penetrating (65.144)
是谓不争之德	this is called the power that comes of not contending (68.151)
报怨以德	to requite injuries with good deeds (79.173)
有德司契	he who has the "power" of Tao is the Grand Almoner (79.173)
无德司彻	he who has not the "power" is the Grand Perquisitor (79.241)

地

天地不仁	Heaven and Earth are ruthless (5.9)
天地之间	Heaven and Earth and all that lies between(5.9)
是为天地根	is the base from which Heaven and Earth sprang (6.11)

恶

斯恶矣	that the idea of ugliness exists (2.3)
美之与恶相去何若	can it be compared to the difference between good and bad (20.40)
物或恶之	people despise them (31.66)

F

法

人法地	the ways of men are conditioned by those of earth (25.51)
地法天	the ways of earth (are conditioned) by those of heaven (25.51)
天法道	the ways of heaven (are conditioned) by those of Tao (25.51)
道法自然	the ways of Tao (are conditioned) by the Self-so (25.51)
法令滋彰	the more laws are promulgated (57.125)

福

祸兮福之所倚	it is upon bad fortune that good fortune leans (58.127)
福兮祸之所伏	upon good fortune that bad fortune rests (58.127)
国之福	bring a stock of good fortune to the land (65.144)

复

吾以观复	I have beheld them, whither they go back

复归其明	return to the inner-light (52. 114)

G

根

天地根	the base from which Heaven and Earth sprang (6. 11)
复归其根	return to the root from which they grew (16. 32)
归根曰静	this return to the root is called Quietness (16. 32)
重为轻根	as the heavy must be the foundation of the light (26. 54)
轻则失根	if he is light, the foundation is lost (26. 54)
深根固柢	making the roots strike deep (59. 129)

功

功成而弗居	achieves his aim, but does not call attention to what he does (2. 3)
功遂身退	when your work is done, then withdraw (9. 17)
功成事遂	when his task is accomplished, his work done (17. 34)
不自伐故有功	he does not boast of what he will do, therefore he succeeds (22. 45)
自伐者无功	he who boasts of what he will do succeeds in nothing (24. 49)
功成而不有	having produced them, it does not take possession of them (34. 72)

	93)
夫轻诺必寡信	light assent inspires little confidence (63.139)
小国寡民	a small country with few inhabitants (80.175)

观

以观其妙	can see the Secret Essences (1.1)
以观其徼	can see only the Outcomes (1.1)
吾以观复	I have beheld them, whither they go back (16.32)
虽有荣观	however magnificent the view (26.54)
以身观身	through oneself one may contemplate Oneself (54.118)
以家观家	through the household one may contemplate the Household (54.118)
以乡观乡	through the village one may contemplate the Village (54.118)
以国观国	through the kingdom one may contemplate the Kingdom (54.118)
以天下观天下	through the empire one may contemplate the Empire (54.118)

归

归根曰静	this return to the root is called Quietness (16.32)
无所归	as though I belonged nowhere (20.40)
诚全而归之	true wholeness can only be achieved by return (22.45)

不以智治国国之福	those who rule without giving knowledge bring a stock of good fortune to the land (65.144)
受国之垢	he who has accepted the dirt of the country (78.171)
受国不祥	he who takes upon himself the evils of the country (78.171)
小国寡民	a small country with few inhabitants (80.175)
领国相望	the next place might be so near at hand (80.175)

H

和

音声相和	pitch and mode give harmony to one another (2.3)
和其光	all glare tempered (4.7)
六亲不和	when the six near ones were no longer at peace (18.36)
冲气以为和	on this blending of the breaths that their harmony depends (42.93)
和之至也	the harmony is at its perfection (55.120)
知和曰常	to understand such harmony is to understand the always-so (55.120)
和其光	all glare tempered (56.123)
和大怨	to allay the main discontent (79.173)

厚

大丈夫处其厚	the full-grown man takes his stand upon

复归于无极	he returns to the Limitless (28.59)
孰知其极	though few know it (58.127)
莫知其极	it knows no bounds (59.129)
莫知其极	only what knows no bounds (59.129)
是谓配天古之极	the secret of being mated to heaven, to what was of old (68.151)

教

行不言之教	carries on wordless teaching (2.3)
人之所教我亦教之	others use in their teaching I too will use in mine (42.93)
吾将以为教父	I will take him for my teacher (42.93)
不言之教	there can be teaching without words (43.96)

静

孰能浊以静之徐清	which of you can assume such murkiness, to become in the end still and clear (15.29)
守静笃	hold fast enough to Quietness (16.32)
归根曰静	this return to the root is called Quietness (16.32)
静曰复命	quietness is called submission to Fate (16.32)
静为躁君	quietness is lord and master of activity (26.54)
不欲以静	to be dispassionate is to be still (37.78)
静胜躁	staying still overcomes heat (movement) (45.100)

国之利器	the State's sharpest weapons (36.76)
带利剑	carry sharp swords (53.116)
不可得而利	cannot be benefited (56.123)
人多利器	the more "sharp weapons" there are (57.125)
或利或害	either may be profitable or unprofitable (73.161)
利而不害	to sharpen without cutting (81.177)

M

美

天下皆知美之为美	it is because every one under Heaven recognizes beauty as beauty (2.3)
美之与恶相去何若	can it be compared to the difference between good and bad (20.40)
胜而不美	the Quietist, even when he conquers, does not regard weapons as lovely things (31.66)
而美之者	for to think them lovely (31.66)
美言可以市尊	there is a traffic in speakers of fine words (62.136)
美其服	pleased with their clothing (80.175)
信言不美	true words are not fine-sounding (81.177)
美言不信	fine-sounding words are not true (81.177)

门

众妙之门	the Doorway whence issued all Secret Es-

民自富	the people will of themselves become prosperous (57.125)
民自朴	the people will of themselves return to the "state of the Uncarved Block" (57.125)
其民淳淳	the people will be happy and satisfied (58.127)
其民缺缺	the people will be carping and discontented (58.127)
民之从事	the people of the world, at their tasks (64.141)
非以明民	not enlighten the people (65.144)
民之难治	the harder they are to rule (65.144)
是以圣人欲上民	the Sage in order to be above the people (66.147)
欲先民	in order to guide them (66.147)
民不重	the people not be crushed by his weight (66.147)
民不害	the people not be led into harm (66.147)
民不畏威	if the people are not intimidated by your authority (72.159)
民不畏死	the people are not frightened of death (74.163)
若民常畏死	even supposing people were generally frightened of death (74.163)
民之饥	the people starve (75.165)
民之难治	the people are difficult to keep in order (75.165)
民之轻死	the people attach no importance to death

	it belongs (25.51)
道常无名	Tao is eternal, but has no fame (name) (32.68)
始制有名	once the block is carved, there will be names (32.68)
名亦既有	so soon as there are names (32.68)
可名为小	it may be called the Lowly (34.72)
可名为大	it is called the Great (34.72)
无名之朴	the blankness of the Unnamed (37.78)
道隐无名	Tao is hidden and nameless (41.90)
名与身	fame or one's own self (44.98)
不见而名	sees all without looking (47.104)
母	
万物之母	the mother that rears the ten thousand creatures (1.1)
贵食母	prize no sustenance that comes not from the Mother's breast (20.40)
为天地母	the mother of all things under heaven (25.51)
为天下母	the"mother"of all things (52.114)
既得其母	apprehends the mother (52.114)
复守其母	hold all the tighter to the mother (52.114)
有国之母	he who having the kingdom goes to the Mother (59.129)

P

朴	
敦兮其若朴	blank, as a piece of uncarved wood (15.

	vessel (29.62)
夫兵者不祥之器	fine weapons are none the less ill-omened things (31.66)
兵者不祥之器	weapons are ill-omened things (31.66)
非君子之器	the superior man should not depend on (31.66)
国之利器	the State's sharpest weapons (36.76)
大器晚成	the Greatest vessel takes the longest to finish (41.90)
人多利器	the "more sharp weapons" there are (57.125)
故能成器长	truly able to become chief of all Ministers (67.149)
什伯之器	contrivances requiring ten times, a hundred times less labour (80.175)

强

强其骨	toughening their sinews (3.5)
故强为之容	I can but tell of them as they appeared to the world (15.29)
强为之名	were I forced to say to what class of things it belongs (25.51)
或强或羸	some are feeling vigorous just when others are worn out (29.62)
不以兵强天下	oppose all conquest by force of arms (30.64)
不敢以取强	he does not take further advantage of his victory (30.64)
果而勿强	fulfils his purpose, but without violence

轻

重为轻根	the heavy must be the foundation of the light (26.54)
以身轻于天下	allow himself to be lighter than these he rules (26.54)
轻则失根	if he is light, the foundation is lost (26.54)
夫轻诺必寡信	light assent inspires little confidence (63.139)
祸莫大于轻敌	the greatest of all calamities is to attack and find no enemy (69.153)
轻敌几丧吾宝	I can have no enemy at the price of losing my treasure (69.153)
民之轻死	the people attach no importance to death (75.165)
是以轻死	that is why they attach no importance to death (75.165)

穷

多言数穷	the force of words is soon spent (5.9)
其用不穷	its use will never fail (45.100)

取

故去彼取此	he rejects that but takes this (12.23)
将欲取天下	those that would gain what is under heaven (29.62)
不敢以取强	he does not take further advantage of his victory (30.64)

	40)
我愚人之心也哉	Mine is indeed the mind of a very idiot, so dull am I (20.40)
俗人昭昭	the world is full of people that shine (20.40)
俗人察察	they look lively and self-assured (20.40)
众人皆有以	all men can be put to some use (20.40)
我独异于人	I most am different from men (20.40)
而况于人乎	how much less in his utterance should man (23.47)
人亦大	so may the ruler (men) also have it (25.51)
人法地	the ways of men are conditioned by those of earth (25.51)
常善救人故无弃人	is all the time in the most perfect way helping men, he certainly does not turn his back on men (27.56)
故善人者不善人之师	the perfect man is the teacher of the imperfect (27.56)
不善人者善人之资	the imperfect is the stock-in-trade of the perfect man (27.56)
以道佐人主者	he who by Tao purposes to help a ruler of men (30.64)
是乐杀人	to delight in the slaughter of men (31.66)
夫乐杀人者	he who delights in the slaughter of men (31.66)
杀人之众	a host that has slain men (31.66)
知人者智	to understand others is to have knowledge (33.70)

善人之宝	it is the treasure of the good man (62.136)
不善人之所保	the support of the bad (62.136)
美行可以加人	persons of grave demeanour are accepted as gifts (62.136)
人之不善何弃之有	even the bad let slip no opportunity to acquire them (62.136)
复众人之所过	turning all men back to the things they have left behind (64.141)
善用人者	the best user of men (68.151)
用人之力	the capacity to use men (68.151)
人之生也柔弱	when he is born, man is soft and weak (76.167)
人之道则不然	far from being man's way (77.169)
而不责于人	not go round making claims on people (79.173)
常与善人	to keep the good perpetually supplied (79.173)
既以为人	his own last scrap has been used up on behalf of others (81.177)
既以与人	his own last scrap has been used up in giving to others (81.177)
人之道	the Sage's way (81.177)

仁

天地不仁	Heaven and Earth are ruthless (5.9)
圣人不仁	the Sage is ruthless (5.9)
与善仁	in friendship they value gentleness (8.15)

	yielding than water (78.171)
柔之胜刚	the soft conquers the hard (78.171)

辱

宠辱若惊	favour and disgrace goad as it were to madness (13.25)
何谓宠辱若惊	what does it mean to say that favour and disgrace goad as it were to madness (13.25)
是谓宠辱若惊	that is what is meant by saying favour and disgrace goad as it were to madness (13.25)
知其荣守其辱	he who knows glory, yet cleaves to ignominy (28.59)
大白若辱	what is sheerest white looks blurred (41.90)
知足不辱	be content with what you have and are, and no one despoil you (44.98)

弱

弱其志	weakening their intelligence (3.5)
将欲弱之	whatever is to be weakened (36.76)
柔弱胜刚强	the soft overcomes the hard, and the weak, the strong (36.76)
弱者道之用	the only useful quality, weakness (40.88)
骨弱筋柔	its bones are soft, its sinews weak (55.120)
人之生也柔弱	when he is born, man is soft and weak

S

三曰不敢为天下先	the third, refusal to be"foremost of all things under heaven"(67.149)

善

皆知善之为善斯不善矣	if evey one recognized virtue as virtue, this would merely create fresh conceptions of wickedness (2.3)
上善若水	the highest good is like that of water (8.15)
水善利万物	the goodness of water is that it benefits the ten thousand creatures (8.15)
居善地	the ground the best place for building a house upon (8.15)
心善渊	thoughts they value those that are profound (8.15)
与善仁	in friendship they value gentleness (8.15)
言善信	in words (they value) truth (8.15)
政善治	in government (they value) good order (8.15)
事善能	in deeds (they value) effectiveness (8.15)
动善时	in actions (they value) timeliness (8.15)
古之善为道者	of old those that were the best officers of Court (15.29)
善行	perfect activity (27.56)
善言	perfect speech (27.56)
善数	perfect reckoner (27.56)
善闭	perfect door (27.56)
善结	perfect knot (27.56)
常善救人	in the most perfect way helping men (27.56)
常善救物	in the most perfect way helping creatures

	(68.151)
善战者不怒	the best fighters do not make displays of wrath (68.151)
善胜敌者不与	the greatest conqueror wins without joining issue (68.151)
善用人者为之下	the best user of men acts as though he were their inferior (68.151)
天之道不争而善胜	it is the way of Heaven not to strive but none the less to conquer (73.161)
不言而善应	not to speak, but none the less to get an answer (73.161)
然而善谋	one who says little, yet none the less has laid his plans (73.161)
安可以为善	can hardly be called successful (79.173)
常与善人	to keep the good perpetually supplied (79.173)
善者不辩	the good man does not prove by argument (81.177)
辩者不善	he who proves by argument is not good (81.177)

上

上善若水	the highest good is like that of water (8.15)
其上不皎	its rising brings no light (14.27)
太上不知有之	of the highest the people merely know that such a one exists (17.34)
恬淡为上	the best attitude is to remain tranquil and

柔弱处上	the soft and weak set on high (76.167)
身	
后其身而身先	puts himself in the background; but is always to the fore (7.13)
外其身而身存	remains outside; but is always there (7.13)
功遂身退天之道	when your work is done, then withdraw (9.17)
贵大患若身	high rank hurts keenly as our bodies hurt (13.25)
何谓贵大患若身	what does it mean to say that high rank hurts keenly as our bodies hurt (13.25)
为吾有身	that we have bodies (13.25)
及吾无身吾有何患	if we had no bodies, how could we suffer (13.25)
贵以身为天下	he who in dealing with the empire regards his high rank as though it were his body (13.25)
爱以身为天下	he who in dealing with the empire loves his subjects as one should love one's body (13.25)
没身不殆	though his body ceases, is not destroyed (16.32)
以身轻于天下	allow himself to be lighter than these he rules (26.54)
名与身孰亲	fame or one's own self, which matters to one most (44.98)
身与货孰多	one's own self or things bought, which

非其神不伤人	nor was it only that his good spirit was not used to harm other men (60.131)

生

有无相生	Being and Not-being grow out of one another (2.3)
生而弗有	he rears them, but does not lay claim to them (2.3)
以其不自生	because they do not foster their own lives (7.13)
故能长生	that is why they live so long (7.13)
生之畜之	rear them, then, feed them (10.19)
生而不有	rear them, but do not lay claim to them (10.19)
孰能安以动之徐生	which of you can make yourself inert, to become in the end full of life and stir (15.29)
先天地生	that existed before heaven and earth (25.51)
荆棘生焉	thorn and brambles grow (30.64)
万物恃之以生	the ten thousand creatures owe their existence to it (34.72)
万物得一以生	the ten thousand creatures (through such understanding) bear their kind (39.84)
万物无以生	were it not that the ten thousand creatures can bear their kind (39.84)
天下万物生于有	all creatures under heaven are the products of Being (40.88)
有生于无	Being itself is the product of Not-being

以其上求生之厚	because those above them are too grossly absorbed in the pursuit of life (75.165)
夫唯无以生为者	in that their hearts are so little set on life
是贤于贵生	they are superior to those who set store by life (75.165)
人之生	when he (man) is born (76.167)
草木之生	while they (all plants and trees) are alive (76.167)
生之徒	a "companion of life" (76.167)

圣人

圣人处无为之事	the Sage relies on actionless activity (2.3)
圣人之治	the Sage rules (3.5)
圣人不仁	the Sage too is ruthless (5.9)
圣人后其身	the Sage puts himself in the background (7.13)
圣人为腹	the Sage considers the belly (12.23)
圣人抱一	the Sage clasps the Primal Unity (22.45)
圣人常善救人	the Sage is all the time in the most perfect way helping men (27.56)
圣人用之	when the Sage uses it (28.59)
圣人去甚	the Sage discards the absolute (29.62)
圣人不行而知	the Sage arrives without going (47.104)
圣人常无心	the Sage has no heart of his own (49.108)
圣人之在天下	the Sage in his dealing with the world (49.108)
圣人皆孩之	the Sage all the time sees and hears no

圣人之道	the Sage's way (81.177)

胜

战胜以丧礼处之	he that has conquered in battle is received with rites of mourning (31.66)
胜人者有力	to conquer others needs strength (33.70)
自胜者强	to conquer oneself is harder still(33.70)
柔弱胜刚强	the soft overcomes the hard, and the weak, the strong (36.76)
静胜躁	movement overcomes cold (45.100)
寒胜热	staying still overcomes heat (45.100)
牝常以静胜牡	the female by quiescence conquers the male (61.133)
夫慈以战则胜	pity cannot fight without conquering (67.149)
善胜敌者不与	the greatest conqueror wins without joining issue (68.151)
哀者胜矣	he who does not delight in war that wins (69.153)
不争而善胜	not to strive but none the less to conquer (73.161)
莫之能胜	not one of them that can prevail (78.171)
弱之能胜	the yielding conquers the resistant (78.171)
柔之胜刚	the soft conquers the hard (78.171)

失

失之若惊	when they lose it they turn distraught

始

无名万物之始	it was from the Nameless that Heaven and Earth sprang (1.1)
能知古始	to know what once there was, in the Beginning (14.27)
始制有名	once the block is carved, there will be names (32.68)
愚之始	it is the beginning of folly (38.80)
天下有始	that which was the beginning of all things under heaven (52.114)
千里之行始于足下	the journey of a thousand leagues began with what was under the feet (64.141)
慎终如始	heed the end no less than the beginning (64.141)

事

圣人处无为之事	the Sage relies on actionless activity (2.3)
事善能	in deeds (they value) effectiveness (8.15)
功成事遂	when his task is accomplished, his work done (17.34)
从事于道者	if one uses the Way as one's instrument (23.47)
其事好还	such things are wont to rebound (30.64)
吉事尚左	in happy events, the left-hand is the place of honour (31.66)
凶事尚右	in grief and mourning, the right-hand is the place of honour (31.66)
常以无事	all did so by not interfering (48.106)

to see (35.74)

长生久视	making life long by fixed staring (59.129)
水	
上善若水	the highest good is like that of water (8.15)
水善利	the goodness of water is that it benefits (8.15)
天之莫柔弱于水	nothing under heaven is softer or more yielding than water (78.171)
损	
故物或损之而益	things are often increased by seeking to diminish them (42.93)
或益之而损	diminished by seeking to increase them (42.93)
为道日损	the practice of Tao consists in substracting day by day (48.106)
损之又损	substracting and yet again substracting (48.106)
有余者损之	take away from those who have too much (77.169)
天之道损有余	it is heaven's way to take from those who have too much (77.169)
损不足	takes away from those that have not enough (77.169)

T

太	
太上不知有之	of the highest the people merely know

天道

天之道	such is Heaven's Way (9.17)
见天道	he knows all the ways of heaven (47.104)
天之道	it is the way of Heaven (73.161)
天之道其犹张弓与	Heaven's way is like the bending of a bow (77.169)
天之道	it is Hcavcn's way (77.169)
天道无亲	it is Heaven's way, without distinction of persons (79.173)
天之道	heaven's way (81.177)

天地

天地之始	that Heaven and Earth sprang (1.1)
天地不仁	Heaven and Earth are ruthless (5.9)
天地之间其犹橐籥乎	Heaven and Earth and all that lies between is like a bellows (5.9)
是谓天地根	is the base from which Heaven and Earth sprang (6.11)
天地所以能长且久者	how come they to be so (7.13)
天地	it is Heaven-and-Earth (23.47)
天地尚不能久	even Heaven-and-Earth cannot blow or pour for long (23.47)
先天地生	that existed before heaven and earth (25.51)
天地相合	Heaven-and-Earth would conspire (32.68)

天下

	all things under heaven (28.59)
为天下谷	and being such a valley (28.59)
将欲取天下	those that would gain what is under heaven (29.62)
天下神器	that which is under heaven is like a holy vessel (29.62)
不以兵强天下	oppose all conquest by force of arms (30.64)
不可得志于天下矣	never get what he looks for out of those that dwell under heaven (31.66)
天下莫能臣	is greater than anything that is under heaven (32.68)
譬道之在天下	to Tao all under heaven will come (32.68)
天下往	goes about his work in the empire (35.74)
天下将自正	the whole empire will be at rest (37.78)
侯王得一以为天下正	barons and princes (through such understanding) direct their people(39.84)
天下之物生于有	all creatures under heaven are the products of Being (40.88)
天下之至柔	what is of all things most yielding (43.96)
驰骋天下之至坚	overwhelm that which is of all things most hard (43.96)
天下希及之	few indeed can understand (43.96)
清净为天下正	he by his limpid calm puts right everything under heaven (45.100)
天下有道	when there is Tao in the empire(46.102)

老子

天下之牝	its part must be that of the female in its dealings with all things under heaven (61.133)
天下之交也	it must be a point towards which all things under heaven converge (61.133)
故为天下贵	most precious of all things under heaven (62.136)
天下难事	everything difficult (63.139)
天下大事	everything great (63.139)
天下乐推	everything under heaven will be glad to be pushed by him (66.147)
故天下莫能与之争	none can contend with him (66.147)
天下皆谓	every one under heaven says (67.149)
不敢为天下先	refusal to be "foremost of all things under heaven" (67.149)
不敢为天下先	he that refuses to be foremost of all things (67.149)
天下莫能知	no one under heaven understands them (70.155)
孰能有余以奉天下	one there is and one only, so rich that he can afford to make offerings to all under heaven (77.169)
天下莫柔弱于水	nothing under heaven is softer or more yielding than water (78.171)
天下莫不知	a fact known by all men (78.171)
是谓天下王	a king among those what dwell under heaven (78.171)

	him (2.3)
万物之宗	the very progenitor of all things in the world (4.7)
以万物为刍狗	the Ten Thousand Things are but as straw dogs (5.9)
水善利万物	the goodness of water is that it benefits the ten thousand creatures (8.15)
万物并作	of the ten thousand things none but can be worked on by you (16.32)
万物将自宾	the ten thousand creatures would flock to do them homage (32.68)
万物恃之以生	the ten thousand creatures owe their existence to it (34.72)
衣养万物	it covers the ten thousand things like a garment (34.72)
万物归焉	the ten thousand creatures obey it (34.72)
万物将自化	the ten thousand creatures would at once be transformed (37.78)
万物得一以生	the ten thousand creatures (through such understanding) bear their kind (39.84)
万物无以生	were it not that the ten thousand creatures can bear their kind (39.84)
三生万物	three things (gave birth) up to ten thousand (42.93)
万物负阴	these ten thousand creatures cannot turn their back to the shade (42.93)
万物莫不尊道	of the ten thousand things there is not one that does not worship Tao (51.112)

	any personal end (7.13)
夫唯不争故无尤	because they prefer what does not lead to strife, and therefore does not go amiss (8.15)
能无离乎	can you...from straying (10.19)
能无疵乎	can you...till all is without blur (10.19)
当其无	it is on the space where there is nothing (11.21)
无之以为用	we should recognize the usefulness of what is not (11.21)
及吾无身	if we had no bodies (13.25)
是谓无状之状	they are called shapeless shapes (14.27)
盗贼无有	thieves and robbers will disappear (19.38)
绝学无忧	banish learning, and there will be no more grieving (19.38)
累累兮若无所归	I droop and drift, as though I belonged nowhere (20.40)
若无止	never brought to a stop (20.40)
自伐者无功	he who boasts of what he will do succeeds in nothing (24.49)
善行无辙迹	perfect activity leaves no track behind it (27.56)
善言无瑕谪	perfect speech is like a jade-worker whose tool leaves no mark (27.56)
善闭无关楗	the perfect door has neither bolt nor bar (27.56)
善结无绳约	the perfect knot needs neither rope nor twine (27.56)
故无弃人	he certainly does not turn his back on

兕无所投其角	a buffalo that attacked him would find nothing for its horns to butt (50. 110)
虎无所措其爪	a tiger would find nothing for its claws to tear (50. 110)
兵无所容其刃	a weapon would find no place for its point to enter in (50. 110)
以其无死地	because such men have no "death-spots" in them (50. 110)
无遗身殃	is thereby preserved from all harm (50. 110)
其无正也	there is a bourn where there is neither right nor wrong (58. 127)
则无不克	it acquires a strength that nothing can overcome (59. 129)
无不克	if there is nothing it cannot overcome (59. 129)
故终无难矣	by doing so avoid all difficulties (63. 139)
圣人无为故无败	the Sage does not act and so does not harm (64. 141)
无执故无失	does not grab, and so does not let slip (64. 141)
则无败事	your work will not be spoiled (64. 141)
是谓行无行	this latter is what we call to march without moving (69. 153)
攘无臂	to roll the sleeve, but present no bare arm (69. 153)
扔无敌	a host that can confront, yet presents no battle-front (69. 153)

我无事而民自富	so long as I act only by inactivity the people will of themselves become prosperous (57.125)
事无事	does without doing (63.139)

无为

圣人处无为之事	the Sage relies no actionless activity (2.3)
为无为则无不治	through his actionless activity all things are duly regulated (3.5)
道常无为而无不为	Tao never does; yet through it all things are done(37.78)
上德无为而无以为	the man of highest "power" neither acts nor is there any who so regards him (38.80)
下德无为而有以为	the man of inferior "power" both acts and is so regarded (38.80)
吾是以知无为之有益	That is how I know the value of action that is actionless (43.96)
无为之益	value in action that is actionless (43.96)
以至于无为	till one has reached inactivity (48.106)
无为而无不为	by this very inactivity, everything can be activated (48.106)
我无为而民自化	so long as I "do nothing" the people will of themselves be transformed (57.125)
为无为	it acts without action (63.139)
圣人无为	the Sage does not act (64.141)

无不为

道常无为而无不为	Tao never does; yet through it all things

	of themselves return to the "state of the Uncarved Block" (57.125)

无知

常使民无知无欲	ever striving to make the people knowledgeless and desireless (3.5)
夫惟无知	because men do not understand this (70.155)

勿

果而勿矜	fulfils his purpose and does not glory in what he has done (30.64)
果而勿伐	fulfils his purpose and does not boast of what he has done (30.64)
果而勿骄	fulfils his purpose, but takes no pride in what he has done (30.64)
果而勿强	fulfils his purpose, but without violence (30.64)

物

复归于无物	on the way back to where there is nothing (14.27)
无物之象	forms without form (14.27)
夫物云云	all things howsoever they flourish (16.32)
道之为物	the Way is a thing (21.43)
其中有物	within it are entities (21.43)
物或恶之	no creature but will reject them in disgust (24.49)

高以下为基	the low is the foundation upon which the high is laid (39.84)
下士闻道	when the man of low capacity hears Tao (41.90)
大邦者下流	a large kingdom must be like the low ground towards which all streams flow down (61.133)
以静为下	by quiescence gets underneath (61.133)
大邦以下小邦	if a large kingdom can in the same way succeed in getting underneath a small kingdom (61.133)
小邦以下大邦	because small kingdoms are by nature in this way underneath large kingdoms (61.133)
故或下以取	the one must get underneath in order to do it (61.133)
或下而取	the other is underneath and therefore does it (61.133)
大者宜为下	the large kingdom must "get underneath" (61.133)
千里之行始于足下	the journey of a thousand leagues began with what was under the feet. (64.141)
以其善下之	through the merit of being lower than they (66.147)
必以言下之	must speak as though he were lower than the people (66.147)
善用人者为之下	the best user of men acts as though he were their inferior (68.151)
强大处下	the hard and mighty are cast down (76.

	greater than anything that is under heaven (32.68)
可名为小	therefore it may be called the Lowly (34.72)
见小曰明	good sight means seeing what is very small (52.114)
治大国若烹小鲜	ruling a large kingdom is indeed like cooking small fish (60.131)
故大邦以下小邦	if a large kingdom can in the same way succeed in getting underneath a small kingdom (61.133)
则取小国	it will win the adherence of the small kingdom (61.133)
小邦以下大邦	small kingdoms are by nature in this way underneath large kingdoms (61.133)
小邦不过欲入事人	what small countries need is some place where their surplus inhabitants can go and get employment (the small nation wants nothing more than to be accepted and serve the large nation) (61.133)
大小多少	make the small great and the few many (63.139)
小国寡民	a small country with few inhabitants (80.175)

心

使民心不乱	their hearts will remain placid and undisturbed (3.5)
虚其心	emptying their hearts (3.5)

	177)
美言不信	fine-sounding words are not true (81.177)

行

行不言之教	carries on wordless teaching (2.3)
令人行妨	impede their owner's movements (12.23)
跨者不行	he who takes the longest strides does not walk the fastest (24.49)
余食赘行	pass round superfluous dishes to those that have already had enough (24.49)
周行而不殆	all pervading, unfailing (25.51)
行不离辎重	he travels all day will not let himself be separated from his baggage-wagon (26.54)
善行无辙迹	perfect activity leaves no track behind it (27.56)
故物或行或随	among the creatures of the world some go in front, some follow (29.62)
强行者有志	he that works through violence may get his way (33.70)
勤而行之	he does his best to put it into practice (41.90)
圣人不行而知	the Sage arrives without going (47.104)
陆行不遇兕虎	he walks on land does not meet tigers or wild buffaloes (50.110)
行于大道	he has got started on the great highway (53.116)
美行可以加人	persons of grave demeanour are accepted

玄

同谓之玄	we can but call the Mystery (1.1)
玄之又玄	rather the "Darker than any Mystery" (1.1)
是谓玄牝	it is named the Mysterious Female (6.11)
玄牝之门	the Doorway of the Mysterious Female (6.11)
涤除玄鉴	wipe and cleanse your vision of the Mystery (10.19)
是谓玄德	this is called the Mysterious Power (10.19)
微妙玄通	subtle, abstruse, mysterious, penetrating (15.29)
是谓玄德	this is called the mysterious power (51.112)
是谓玄同	this is called the mysterious levelling (56.123)
是谓玄德	is called the mysterious "power" (65.144)
玄德深矣	the mysterious "power," so deep-penetrating (65.144)

Y

一

载营魄抱一	keep the unquiet physical-soul from straying, holding fast to the Unity (10.19)
三十辐共一毂	put thirty spokes together and call it a

先义而后礼	after morality was lost, then came ritual (38.80)

益

物或损之而益	things are often increased by seeking to diminish them (42.93)
或益之而损	and diminished by seeking to increase them (42.93)
无为之有益	the value of action that is actionless (43.96)
无为之益	value in action that is actionless (43.96)
为学日益	learning consists in adding to one's stock day by day (48.106)
益生曰祥	to fill life to the brim is to invite omens (55.120)

盈

用之或不盈	be drawn from without ever needing to be filled (4.7)
持而盈之	stretch a bow to the very full (9.17)
不欲盈	not try to fill themselves to the brim (15.29)
夫唯不盈	because they do not try to fill themselves to the brim (15.29)
洼则盈	to become full, be hollow (22.45)
谷得一以盈	the abyss (through such understanding) is replenished (39.84)
谷无以盈	were it (the abyss) not for this replenishment (39.84)

太上不知有之	of the highest the people merely know that such a one exists (17.34)
信不足焉有不信	it is by not believing people that you turn them into liars (17.34)
大道废有仁义	it was when the Great Way declined that human kindness and morality arose (18.36)
智慧出有大伪	it was when intelligence and knowledge appeared that the Great Artifice began (18.36)
六亲不和有孝慈	it was when the six near ones were no longer at peace that there was talk of "dutiful sons" (18.36)
国家昏乱有忠臣	nor till fatherland was dark with strife did we hear of "loyal slaves" (18.36)
绝巧弃利盗贼无有	banish skill, discard profit, and thieves and robbers will disappear (19.38)
故令有所属	then let them have accessories (19.38)
众人皆有余	all men have enough and to spare (20.40)
众人皆有以	all men can be put to some use (20.40)
其中有象	latent in it are forms (21.43)
其中有物	within it are entities (21.43)
其中有精	within it there is a force (21.43)
其精甚真其中有信	a force that though rarefied is none the less efficacious (21.43)
不自伐故有功	he does not boast of what he will do, therefore he succeeds (22.45)
信不足焉有不信	it is by not believing in people that you turn them into liars (23.47)

有生于无	Being itself is the product of Not-being (40.88)
故建言有之	therefore the proverb has it (41.90)
无有入无间	being substanceless it can enter even where there is no space (43.96)
吾是以知无为之有益	that is how I know the value of action that is actionless (43.96)
天下有道	when there is Tao in the empire (46.102)
及其有事不足以取天下	had they interfered, they would never have won this adherence (48.106)
生之徒十有三	if the "companions of life" are thirteen (three-tenths) (50.110)
死之徒十有三	so likewise are the "companions of death" thirteen (three-tenths) (50.110)
人之生动之于死地亦十有三	the "death-spots" in man's life and activity are also thirteen (those who could have lived long but walk into death of their own accord also number about three-tenths) (50.110)
生而不有	rear them, but not lay claim to them (51.112)
天下有始	that which was the beginning of all things under heaven (52.114)
使我介然有知	he who has the least scrap of sense (53.116)
财货有余	have more possessions than they can use (53.116)
法令滋彰盗贼多有	the more laws are promulgated, the more

人之道损不足而补有余	being man's way, he takes away from those that have not enough in order to make offering to those who have too much (77.169)
孰能有余以奉天下唯有道者	one there is and one only, so rich that he can afford to make offerings to all under heaven, it is the possessor of Tao (77.169)
必有余怨	only in a manner that will certainly produce further discontents (79.173)
有德司契	he who has the "power" of Tao is the Grand Almoner (79.173)
使有什伯之器	there should be among the people contrivances requiring ten times, a hundred times less labour (80.175)
虽有舟舆	there might still be boats and carriages (80.175)
虽有甲兵	there might still be weapons of war (80.175)
既以为人己愈有	when his own last scrap has been used up on behalf of others, lo, he has more than before (81.177)

欲

常无欲以观其妙	he that rids himself forever of desire can see the Secret Essences (1.1)
常有欲以观其徼	he that has never rid himself of desire can see only the Outcomes (1.1)
不见可欲	if the people never see such things as ex-

	inhabitants (61.133)
小邦不过欲入事人	what small countries need is some place where their surplus inhabitants can go and get employment (61.133)
夫两者各得所欲	each gets what it needs (61.133)
圣人欲不欲	the Sage wants only things that are unwanted (64.141)
圣人欲上民	the Sage in order to be above the people (66.147)
欲先民必以身后之	in order to guide them he must put himself behind them (66.147)
其不欲见贤	because he does not wish to reveal himself as better than others (77.169)

渊

渊兮似万物之宗	it is bottomless; the very progenitor of all things in the world (4.7)
心善渊	among thoughts they value those that are profound (8.15)
鱼不可脱于渊	it is best to leave the fish down in his pool (36.76)

Z

长

长而不宰	be chief among them, but do not manage them (10.19)
圣人用之则为官长	when the Sage uses it, it becomes Chief of all Ministers (28.59)
长之育之	made them grow, fostered them (51.

	zes beauty as beauty (2.3)
皆知善之为善	equally if every one recognized virtue as virtue (2.3)
常使民无知无欲	ever striving to make the people knowledgeless and desireless (3.5)
吾不知谁之子	was it too the child of something else? we cannot tell (4.7)
爱民治国能无为乎	can you love the people and rule the land, yet remain unknown (10.19)
能知古始是谓道纪	to know what once there was, in the Beginning, this is called the essence of the Way (14.27)
知常曰明	to know the always-so is to be illumined (16.32)
不知常妄作凶	not to know it, means to go blindly to disaster (16.32)
知常容	he who knows the always-so has room in him for everything (16.32)
太上不知有之	of the highest the people merely know that such a one exists (17.34)
吾何以知众甫之状哉	how do I know that the many warriors are so (21.43)
吾不知其名	its true name we do not know (25.51)
知其雄守其雌	he who knows the male, yet cleaves to what is female (28.59)
知其白守其黑	he who knows the white, yet cleaves to the black (28.59)
知其荣守其辱	he who knows glory, yet cleaves to ignominy (28.59)

	the tighter to the mother (52.114)
使我介然有知	he who has the least scrap of sense (53.116)
吾何以知天下然哉	how do I know that the empire is so (54.118)
未知牝牡之合	not yet to have known the union of male and female (55.120)
知和曰常	to understand such harmony is to understand the always-so (55.120)
知常曰明	to understand the always-so is to be illumined (55.120)
知者不言	those who know do not speak (56.123)
言者不知	those who speak do not know (56.123)
吾何以知其然哉	how do I know that it is so (57.125)
孰知其极	though few know it (58.127)
无不克则莫知其极	if there is nothing it cannot overcome, it knows no bounds (59.129)
莫知其极可以有国	only what knows no bounds is huge enough to keep a whole kingdom in its grasp (59.129)
知此两者亦稽式	to have understood the difference between these two things is to have a test and standard (65.144)
常知稽式是谓玄德	to be always able to apply this test and standard is called the mysterious "power" (65.144)
吾言甚易知甚易行	my words are very easy to understand and very easy to put into practice (70.155)
天下莫能知莫能行	no one under heaven understands them;

	are kept (57.125)
治人事天莫若啬	you cannot rule men nor serve heaven unless you have laid up a store (59.129)
治大国若烹小鲜	ruling a large kingdom is indeed like cooking small fish (60.131)
治之于未乱	put them in order before they have got into confusion (64.141)
民之难治以其智多	the more knowledge people have, the harder they are to rule (65.144)
故以智治国	those who seek to rule by giving knowledge (65.144)
不以智治国	those who rule without giving knowledge (65.144)
民之难治以其上之有为	the people are difficult to keep in order because those above them interfere (75.165)
是以难治	that is the only reason why they are so difficult to keep in order (75.165)

智

使夫智者不敢为也	indeed he sees to it that if there be any who have knowledge they dare not interfere (3.5)
智慧出有大伪	when intelligence and knowledge appeared that the Great Artifice began (18.36)
绝圣弃智	banish wisdom, discard knowledge (19.38)
虽智大迷	much learning though he may possess, is

	(66.147)
使民重死	the people would be ready to lay down their lives (80.175)

主

万乘之主	the lord of ten thousand chariots (26.54)
以道佐人主者	he who by Tao purposes to help a ruler of men (30.64)
不为主	makes no claim to be master over them (34.72)
万物归焉而不为主	the ten thousand creatures obey it, though they know not that they have a master (34.72)
吾不敢为主	when you doubt your ability to meet the enemy's attack (69.153)
是谓社稷主	can become a king among those what dwell under heaven (78.171)

自

以其不自生	it is because they do not foster their own lives (7.13)
自遗其咎	that brings ruin in its train (9.17)
自今及古	from the time of old till now (21.43)
不自见故明	he does not show himself; therefore he is seen everywhere (22.45)
不自是故彰	he does not define himself, therefore he is distinct (22.45)
不自伐故有功	he does not boast of what he will do, therefore he succeeds (22.45)

	"state of the Uncarved Block" (57.125)
自知不自见	knows himself but does not show himself (72.159)
自爱不自贵	knows his own value, but does not put himself on high (72.159)
不召而自来	not to beckon; yet things come to it of themselves (73.161)

自化

万物将自化	the ten thousand creatures would at once be transformed (37.78)
我无为而民自化	so long as I "do nothing" the people will of themselves be transformed (57.125)

自然

我自然	it happened of its own accord (17.35)
希言自然	to be always talking is against nature (23.47)
道法自然	the ways of Tao (are conditioned) by the Self-so (25.51)
常自然	it was always and of itself so (51.112)
以辅万物之自然	the ten thousand creatures may be restored to their Self-so (64.141)

注释 Notes

Chapter 1

1 For these two sentences, there are usually two different interpretations. In Wang Bi text, they are read as"无名,天地之始;有名,万物之母", thus Waley's translation follows it, which is different from Wang Anshi text as "有,名天地之始;有,名万物之母",the translation should be"'Non-being' names this beginning of Heaven and Earth;'Being' names the mother of the myriad things"by Rhett Young and Roger Ames.

2 The usual understanding of these two sentences should be "From eternal non-existence, therefore, we serenely observe the mysterious beginning of the Universe; From eternal existence we clearly see the apparent distinctions"by Chu Dagao.

3 For"玄之又玄",there are different translations, for instance, "More mystical than the most mystical"by Paul Lin;"even more profound than the profound"by Robert Henricks.

4 As to "众妙之门",we can take for reference that "the gate of all mysteries" by Young and Ames; and"gate whence comes the beginning of all parts of the Universe"by Chu Dagao.

Chapter 2

1 Some people interpret these two sentences as"天下都知道美之为美,就成了丑;天下都知道善之为善,就成了恶" which is translated as"The whole world recognizes the beautiful as beautiful, yet this is only the ugly; the whole world recognizes the good as the good, yet this is only the bad"by D. C. Lau.

2 The accepted translation for"善"is goodness, and "德", virtue; while in Waley's translation they are virtue and power respectively.

3 Gao Heng suspects this"therefore" was added by some later scholar for the lines above are not consistent in style and meaning with the following. The first part is on relativity, and the second on government.

4 Chen Guying holds that the proper word for"无为" should be non-action translated by W. T. Chan. Chan explains, "Non-action (wuwei) is not meant literally'inactivity'but rather 'taking no action that is contrary to Nature' in other words, letting Nature take its own course." (A Source Book in Chinese Philosophy P. 98)

5 For "万物作而弗始", we can take for reference that "He lets all things rise without dominating them" by Paul Lin and "The Sage permits the myriad things to arise of themselves, but does not attempt to be their master" by Rhett Young and Roger Ames.

Chapter 3

1 The accepted translation for “贤” is “the worthy,” “men of worth” or“ superiormen.”

2 For “虚其心”, W. T. Chan explains, “Literally, ‘empty’ (hsu) means absolute peace and purity of mind, freedom from worry and selfish desires.”

Chapter 4

1 “似万物之宗”, this sentence can be translated in different ways such as “as if it were the first ancestor of the myriad things” by Young and Ames, “it is like the ancestor of the myriad creatures” by D. C. Lau.

2 The lines in parentheses belong to Chapter 56.

3 This sentence “湛兮,似或存” is regarded consistent in syntactic structure with “渊兮! 似万物之宗”, thus English translation can be “In its profundity it seems to be the origin of all things. In its depth it seems ever to remain” by Chu Dagao.

4 Waley thinks that “The Ancestor (帝) in question is almost certainly the Yellow Ancestor who seperated Earth from Heaven and destroyed the Primal Unity,” but Wang Bi says, “it is God in heaven.” So the different versions are provided here for reference, “it images the forefather of God” by D. C. Lau, “But it looks like the predecessor of Nature” by Chu Dagao, and “It seems to be the predecessor of the gods” by Young and Ames.

Chapter 5

1 Wang Bi says, "Heaven and Earth follow a natural course and accord with non-ction and non-creation, the myriad things grow and die of their own accord, thus Heaven and Earth are ruthless." Chen Guying explains, "天地不仁" means that Heaven and Earth are without favourites. That is, Heaven and Earth are only a physical and natural existence, and do not possess any human emotions. The myriad things between Heaven and Earth simply comply with the natural law. However, theists think Heaven and Earth show particular favour (rejection) towards some things. In fact, this is only the projection of human sentiments onto the cosmic order.

2 "刍狗" is a dog-like figure made of straw, used usually for sacrificial ceremony. Lin Xiyi says, "The straw dogs are made for the occasion of sacrifice, when it is finished, they are abandoned. The analogy shows they receive no particular favour and are easily forgotten… Some scholars explain this sentence as treating people as straws, certainly they are mistaken."

3 Paul Lin remarks, "The Sage, joining in the virtue of Heaven and Earth, compares the people to straw dogs."

4 According to Yan Lingfeng, "守中" should be "守冲", so this sentence may be translated as "Is it not better to keep tranquility".

Chapter 6

1 Yan Fu explains, "Because it is empty, it is called 'va-

lley'; because it is changeable and inexhaustible, it is called 'spirit'; because it changes unceasingly, it 'never dies'." (Comments and A Textual Study of Dao De Jing)

2 "玄牝" here refers to the creative nature of Tao. It (the valley spirit) gives birth to Heaven, Earth and myriad things but there is nowhere to find the primordial womb.

3 For the last two sentences, we can take for reference that "Perpetual and without end is its invisible existence; Its functions are inexhaustible"; and "Dimly visible, it seems as if it were there, Yet use will never drain it" by D. C. Lau.

Chapter 7

1 Robert Henricks translated these two sentences as "The reason why Heaven and Earth can endure and last a long time—Is that they do not live for themselves."

2 In some Chinese editions, the two words are "长久", there can be subtle difference for the rendition as "they are able to remain perpetually existent" by Young and Ames.

3 A better version can be like that "Put self-concern out of his mind, yet finds that his self-concern is preserved" by Robert Henricks.

4 An alternative translation can be that "Is it not because of his selflessness that he completes his own" by Paul Lin.

Chapter 8

1 Heshang Gong says, "Men of supreme goodness resemble the nature of water."

2 D. C. Lau put these seven sentences as:

In a home it is the site that matters;
In quality of mind it is depth that matters;
In an ally it is benevolence that matters;
In speech it is good faith that matters;
In government it is order that matters;
In affairs it is ability that matters;
In action it is timeliness that matters.

Chapter 9

1 Waley's note: The expression used can also apply to filling a vessel to the brim, but "stretching a bow" makes a better parallel to "sharpening a sword."

2 It should be "gold".

3 Wang Zhen comments, "'身退' does not mean one should retire from his office and leave, but does not claim the deed for himself."

4 Paul Lin explains, "The four seasons evolve in turn, each completing its role and then moving on."

Chapter 10

1 Fan Yingyuan explains, "'营魄' are spiritual and sentient souls." The Book of Internal Perception says, "What controls the body in movement is the spiritual soul, whereas what keeps the body in tranquility is the sentient soul."

2 Chen Guying changed this word "玄览" to "玄鉴" based on the Silk Text B and Gao Heng's explanation. A possible

translation for it can be "Profound mirror".

3 This is a good translation, but other versions can provide us with some reference as "Can you love the people and govern the state by non-action" by Chu Dagao; and "One should love his people and order the country properly, But can he accord with 'non-action'" by Young and Ames.

4 The sentences in parentheses are repeated in Chapter 51, they are irrelevant in meaning to the text above.

Chapter 11

1 This sentence can be translated as "Thirty spokes unite in one hub" by Henricks.

2 We can take the following for reference, "Therefore, on the one hand we have the benefit of existence, and on the other, we make use of non-existence" by Chu Dagao, and "Therefore, being constitutes utility, While non-being constitutes function" by Young and Ames.

Chapter 12

1 Excessive riding and hunting cause one to lose his sense of restraint.

2 "That" refers to a life "on behalf of what the eyes desire", while "this", a life "on behalf of what the stomach needs".

Chapter 13

1 This sentence is better understood as "Concern keenly for one's body as one does for a greater disaster."

2 This sentence should read as "Favour is an inferior matter, if one gets..."

3 Young and Ames translated the sentence as "when one can govern the empire with the same attitude as he esteems his own person."

Chapter 14

1 Alternative translations can be "Its surface is not dazzling bright, Nor is its underside dark," by Young and Ames, and "Its upper part is not dazzling, Its lower part is not obscure" by D. C. Lau.

Waley's notes:

2 i. e. dominate.

3 Macrocosmically, in the Universe. Microcosmically, in oneself.

4 Literally, main-thread.

5 Different translations can be read as "By adhering to the Tao of the past You will master the existence of the present And be able to know the origin of the past. This is called the clue of Tao" by Chu Dagao; "Grasp the Tao of antiquity to superintend present existence: Being able to understand the beginning of the universe Is called the major principle of the Tao" by Young and Ames.

Chapter 15

1 In Wang Bi text, it is "士", but in Silk Manuscript Text B and Fu Yi text, it is "道". Therefore, in Chen Guyin text it is "善为道者", the perfect man of Tao.

2 "澹兮其若海,兮若无止" is moved from the twentieth chapter to follow this sentence according to the explanation given by Yan Lingfeng.

3 Young and Ames' translation for the last four sentences may provide for the reference: "Who is able to slowly become perspicacious through tranquility while dwelling in a situation of turbidity? Who is able to slowly advance through motion while dwelling in a situation of stability? Those who maintain these principles do not seek self-satisfaction. Only because they are not self-satisfied are they able to be rejuvenating."

Chapter 16

1 In Wang Bi text it is "kingly" (王), but his comment is "Nothing is not encompassed." So according to Lao Jian, we should adopt "complete" (全) here.

2 "天" here should be "nature," so the sentence can be translated as "To be complete is to be in accord with nature."

3 A proper translation will be that "to the end of his days, he will suffer no harm".

Chapter 17

1 In Wang Bi text, it is "the people merely know"(下知有之), but in many other texts, such as Wu Cheng's, Zhu Yuanzhang's, Jiao Hong's, etc. it is "people do not know"(不知有之) which is consistent with the overall text and Laozi's philosophy.

2 A different rendition is that "When trust is insufficient, there will be no trust in return" by Robert Henricks.

Chapter 18

1 "仁义" is often translated as benevolence and righteousness.

2 Waley's note: father, son, elder brother, younger brother, husband and wife.

3 "孝慈" is usually translated as "filial piety and parental affection".

4 Waley's note: As Ministers called themselves.

Chapter 19

1 The first sentence of the twentieth chapter should be moved here. Gao Heng explains: This sentence belongs to Chapter 19, it can be verified at three points. Firstly, the similar syntactical structure between "banish learning and have no anxiety", "manifest simplicity and embrace genuinness" and "lessen self-interest and abate desires", it is quite different from

other sentences in structure in Chapter 20; secondly, the same rhyme for "忧" with "足、属、朴、欲", but there is not any other word with the same rhyme in Chapter 20; thirdly, "manifest simplicity and embrace genuineness" is consistent in the meaning with "banish learning and have no anxiety", but if this sentence is put at the beginning of the twentieth chapter, the meaning seems irrelevant to the following sentences.

Chapter 20

1 According to Chen Guying, wei (唯) is the response made when a junior replies to an elder, while o (阿) is the response made when an elder replies to a junior. Some commentators consider that the word 阿 is a loanword for "to shout", "to scold" (诃), and thus explain it as a word of reproach.

2 This sentence should be understood as "Vast (is my spirit), as though interminate".

3 It should be "to be insufficient".

4 See Chapter 15.

5 Waley's note: i. e. the Way's. The image may equally well be that of a child in the womb, "feeding on the mother".

Chapter 21

1 "精" is usually translated as "essence", the most subtle and most fundamental substance.

2 According to Chen Guying's comment, these last four lines should be understood as "Its name has not been abandoned in discerning the origin of all things. How do I know the disposi-

tion of this origin of the myriad things? From it (the Way)."

Chapter 22

1 Waley's note: To the Way.

Chapter 23

1 Waley's note: Nature, as we should say.

2 Here it should be "the Way and its virtue."

3 See Chapter 17. Young and Ames translated this sentence as "When the integrity (of the ruler) is inadequate, There will be those who do not trust him."

Chapter 24

1 This sentence is often understood as "He who puts himself on display does not shine."

2 Waley's note: Over the scene of his successes, thus calling attention to them.

Chapter 25

1 Waley's note: Returning to "what was there at the Beginning."

2 Waley's note: Henceforward I shall use the Chinese word Tao instead of the Way, to do so avoids many inconvenience.

3 In Fan Yingyuan and Fu Yi texts, this word is "man." If we take the whole text into consideration, we would think "man"

is a better choice.

4 Waley's note: The "unconditioned"; the "what-is-so-itself".

Chapter 26

1 In Chen Guying text, it is explained as "luxurious life."

2 Waley's note: i. e. more easily moved.

3 Waley's note: i. e. Quietness, the magical passivity that is also called non-action.

4 For the last two sentences, Young and Ames' translation reads as "If he is flippant he will lose the root; If he is agitated he will lose the way of being a ruler."

Chapter 27

1 According to Chen Guying, this sentence should be "A good traveller leaves no track" by Henricks.

2 i. e. counting sticks or tallies.

3 This is called "according with natural perspicacity" by Young and Ames.

4 D. C. Lau puts these two sentences as "Hence the good man is the teacher the bad learns from; And the bad man is the material the good works on."

5 Waley's note: The power to influence mankind through Tao. The commonest charge brought against Taoists was that of being merely interested in self-perfection without regard for the welfare of the community as a whole. The present chapter is devoted to rebutting that charge.

Chapter 28

1 The comments by Yi Shunding, Ma Xunlun and Gao Heng state that the sentences within the parentheses are probably the addition by later scholars.

2 Waley's note: Play on the double sense of this word which also means "a subordinate", "an instrument of government".

3 Waley's note: Play on "制", "to carve" and "to rule". The secondary meaning is that the greatest ruler does the least chopping about.

Chapter 29

1 "天下" here means people under heaven.

2 Yi Shunding says, "After 'dangerous to temper with' there should be another sentence 'impossible to grab at', I can list three examples to verify this. In the note to the Introduction to Historyof Jin Dynasty by Gan Bao, Li Shan quotes from Wenzi, 'Laozi says, "The world is great vessel, it cannot be grabbed at, and dangerous to temper with. He who tempers with it. damages it; he who grabs at it, lost it."' This is the first. Wang Bi in his notes says, 'Therefore, they can be accorded with but not tempered with; they can be understood but not grabbed at.' Since Wang Bi quotes this sentence in his comment, we can be sure there is such a sentence in the original text. This is the second. In Chapter 64, we read, 'He who acts, harms; he who grabs, lets slip. Therefore, the Sage does not act, and so does

not harm; Does not grab, and so does not let slip.' 'Does not act' means 'cannot be tempered with'; 'does not grab' means 'impossible to grab at'. Thus in Chapter 29, there is such a sentence. This is the third proof."

3 The sentences in parentheses are suspected to be misplaced bamboo slips in Chapter 64, according to Xi Dong, they are moved here.

4 Chen Guying explains "物" as man.

5 This sentence should be "discards the extreme, the extravagant, the excessive".

Chapter 30

1 Waley's note: Lit. "To be reversed." He who overcomes by violence will himself be overcome by violence.

Chapter 31

1 Chen Guying revised "fine weapons" to "weapons" based on Silk Texts A and B.

2, 3, 4 For this chapter, Waley held that a considerable amount of commentary had been inextricably confused with the text. So he reconstructed the text which was fairly close to that of Ma Xulun (1924). The sentences in the parentheses are my additions based on Chen Guying text with the reference of different translations.

Chapter 32

1 For the beginning sentences, we can take for reference that "The way is for ever nameless. Though the uncarved block is small, No one in the world dare claim its allegiance" by D. C. Lau; and "The Tao is an eternally nameless genuinness. Although its manifestations are subtle, There is no one in the empire capable of making it his minister" by Young and Ames.

2 According to Chen Guying, this sentence should be translated as "There is no need for the people to command it, for it is equally distributed of its own accord."

3 Waley's note: i. e. to the possessor of Tao. The last two lines resume the thought of lines 4 and 5.

Chapter 33

1 "Violence" should be replaced with "tenacity" or "perseverance".

Chapter 34

1 Chu Takao's translation for this two sentences is "The great Tao pervades everywhere, both on the left and on the right."

2 "衣被" (to cover…like a garment) now in Chen Guying text is "衣养", which means "to clothe and nourish".

3 The parentheses are added to show that this sentence possibly was inserted by later scholars.

Chapter 35

1 Waley's comment: The Great Form that is formless, i. e. Tao.

2 According to Chen Guying, these first four lines should be translated as "Hold fast to the Great Form, and all the world will throng to you; They will throng to you, and yet will inflict no injury on each other; All will find contentment in concord and equanimity" by Young and Ames.

Chapter 36

1 It should be "subtle but clear" in the light of Fan Yingyuan's comment.

2 Different explanations for "利器": Heshang Gong thinks it is the principle of authority; Han Fei believes it means rewards and punishments; Fan Yingyuan explicates it as sagacity, wisdom, benevolence, righteousness, artfulness and profits.

3 Young and Ames translated this sentence as "The sharp weapons of the state cannot be indiscriminately flaunted before the people."

Chapter 37

1 It should be "would be transformed of their own accord," "at once" is redundant here.

2 Waley's note: Literally, "the uncarven-wood-quality".

3 According to Gao Heng, "镇之以" should be added to the

beginning of this sentence, so the English translation should be added with "Refrain them by".

4 Consequently, this sentence should be "they will free from avarice".

5 Waley's note: If the sage is "still".

Chapter 38

1 Waley's note: Does not act separately and particularly, but only applie, the "power" in a general way.

2 Waley's note: Regards him as possessor of power.

3 It should be "chaos".

4 A great man. Waley's note: Full grown in Tao.

Chapter 39

1 "寡" means "friendly", "不穀" means "unworthy" here.

2 In Chen Guying text, this sentence is "至誉无誉", That is, "highest praise is to be without praise." In Wang Bi text, it is "至舆无舆".

3 Waley's note: The sage of old.

4 This sentence may be understood like this: They would rather be like firm and jagged stones than like the glittering and dazzling precious jade.

Chapter 40

1 Chen Guying explains, "The meaning of non-being in this sentence is the same as that 'Non-being names this beginning of

Heaven and Earth' in Chapter 1, but different from that 'Being and non-being grow out of one another' in Chapter 2 and that 'it is on the space where there is nothing that the usefulness of the wheel depends' in Chapter 11. The '无' in Chapters 2 and 11 refers to non-concrete and intangible aspect of phenomenal world, whereas '无' in this chapter refers to the metaphysical Tao. '有' and '无' in Chapters 2 and 11, if translated into English, '有' is equivalent to 'existence', '无' is equivalent to 'non-existence'. However, '有' and '无' in this chapter and Chapter 1 are untranslatable, but if we are forced to translate them, usually, they are 'being' and 'non-being' respectively. (But, we must not confuse them with Parmenides' concepts of being and non-being, for Parmenides, there is only one unchanging, unmoving and indivisible real existence, he calls it 'being', but there is no non-being for him.) Laozi pays attention both to being and non-being and holds their relation as complementary and continuous."

Chapter 41

1 Waley's note: Tao.

2 This sentence should be put after the sentence "What is in its natural, pure state looks faded" according to Zhang Songru.

Chapter 42

1 Waley's note: i. e. everything.

2 Waley's note: Which symbolizes the fact that they are themselves a mixture of light and dark, hard and soft, water and

fire, etc.

3 See Chapter 39.

4 This chapter is divided into two paragraphs, but the meaning in the second paragraph seems irrelevant to the first. Gao Heng, Chen Zhu and Yan Lingfeng suspect the second paragraph belongs to Chapter 39.

Chapter 44

1 Waley's note: i. e. which is better, to get fame and wealth but injure oneself, or to lack fame and wealth and save oneself.

2 Young and Ames' translation will provide for our reference that "one who cherishes reputation to excess must certainly pay a heavy penalty".

Chapter 45

1 According to Jiang Xichang's commentary, these two lines should be "still overcomes movement, and cold overcomes heat".

2 In accordance with Chen Guying's explanation, Young and Ames translated this sentence as "Clarity and tranquility become the upright models of the empire."

Chapter 46

1 There is no such sentence in Wang Bi and Chen Guying texts, but in the texts of Heshang Gong, Fu Yi, Fan Yingyuan,

Jinglong Tablet, the Mawangdui Silk Manuscript Text A and B. Waley also translated this sentence. Therefore I add this sentence to Chen Guying text.

Chapter 47

1 Waley's note: Away from Tao; away from the Unity into the Multiplicity.

Chapter 48

1 We can take D. C. Lau's translation as reference: "In the pursuit of learning one knows more every day; In the pursuit of the way one does less every day. One does less and less until one does nothing at all, and when one does nothing at all there is nothing that is undone."

Chapter 49

1 Waley's note: Makes no judgements of his own.

2 It should be "common people".

3 The sentence can be revised as "the Sage regards them all as infants".

Chapter 50

1 This sentence can be revised as "Human life begins in birth, and ends in death."

2 Waley's note: "The four limbs and nine apertures that

constitute the human apparatus." This is based on the explanation of Han Feizi. Actually, "十有三" should be "three-tenths."

3 The meaning for this sentence could be that "Those who could have lived long but walk into death of their own accord also number about three-tenths."

4 It is "rhinoceros".

Chapter 51

1 For the third and forth lines, we may take for reference the translation "The physical world gives form to them, and their environment completes them" by Young and Ames.

2 It should be "stablized and pacified."

3 For this sentence, different translations can be taken as reference: "It does things to assist them" by Young and Ames; "It benefits them" by D. C. Lau; and "It acts on their behalf" by Henricks.

4 See Chapter 10.

Chapter 52

Waley's note:

1 Tao, the One, the Whole.

2 the Many, the universe.

3 i. e. Tao.

Chapter 53

1 Waley's note: All this is of course metaphorical.

2 A different understanding for "除" is "to be rank with corruption."

Chapter 54

Waley's note:

1 Literally "what is well planted," i. e. planted by Tao.

2 The "power" of the ancestor' Tao carries the family on.

3 By delving back through the successive stages of one's own conscious one gets back to the Unity of the Whole which is one's Tao.

4 Waley's note: i. e. the Tao of the household. When one has had vision of the Tao (underlying essence) of a thing, one can control it. This catena (self-household-village, etc.) is found in every branch of Chinese philosophy, applied in a variety of ways.

Chapter 55

1 The usual understanding for this sentence should be that "He who is endowed with ample virtue may be compared to an infant" by Chu Dagao, and that "One who possesses virtue in abundance is comparable to a new born babe" by D. C. Lau.

2 For these two sentences, Chu Dagao translates them as "To know this harmony is to approach eternity; To know eternity is to attain enlightenment."

老

子

Chapter 56

1 See Chapter 52,

2 Waley's note: In which there is a general perception not effected through particular senses.

Chapter 57

1 It is "unexpected manoeuvres."

2 Principle of Tao.

Chapter 58

1 Young and Ames' translation for the first two lines: "When the goveminent is dull and sluggish, The people will be simple and sincere."

2 Waley's note: Through Tao he reaches his ends without use of means. To translate "shines without dazzling" is to misunderstand the whole sequence.

Chapter 59

1 Although "事天" literally can be translated as "serve heaven," in fact, it means "nurture one's own person," Wang Chunfu says, "serving heaven" means to fulfill that which has been endowed by Heaven, which in turn means "nurturing one's own person."

2 According to Chen Guying, this means frugality or thrift-

ness.

3 Waley's note: i. e. going to Tao the Mother.

4 In Chen Guying text, "久视" means "to increase one's span of existence."

Chapter 60

1 Simply, gods or spirits.

2 Waley's understanding is different from that of Chen Guying's. According to Chen, this sentence can be translated as "also the sage will not injure others."

Chapter 61

1 In Silk Manuscript Text A, the third sentence is before the second sentence.

2 It should be "the protection".

3 For the sentences in the parentheses, the correct translation should be that "The large nation wants nothing more than to ally and nurture the people, While the small nation wants nothing more than to be accepted by and to serve the large nation" by Young and Ames.

Chapter 62

1 Waley's note: Where family worship was carded on; the pivotal point round which the household centered. This sentence is translated as "the sanctuary of the thousand things" by Young and Ames.

2 It is"three high ministers,"i. e. the Grand Tutor, Deputy Grand Tutor, and Senior Guardian of the Heir-Apparent.

Chapter 63

1 Some scholars suspect there are missing words here, for it is difficult to explain the sentence. Duyvendak put in English as: "to consider what is small as great, and a few as many."

2 This sentence is not fit for the context, according to Ma Xulun and Yan Lingfeng, it is moved to Chapter 79.

Chapter 64

1 See Chapter 29.

2 Chen Guying holds the sentences in the parentheses do not belong to this chapter, bacause their meaning are not consistent with those above.

Chapter 65

1 For "稽式", D. C. Lau translates it as "models," and Young and Ames put it as "principles."

Chapter 66

1 For"推", D. C. Lau translates it as"support,"and Young and Ames as"promote."

Chapter 67

1 The sentences in the parentheses are not relevant in meaning to the following, so Yan Lingfeng thinks they can be moved to the end of Chapter 34.

2 Waley's note: The three rules that formed the practical, political side of the author's teaching—(1) abstention from aggressive was and capital punishment, (2) absolute simplicity of living, (3) refusal to assert active authority.

3 A different rendition will be "the leader of all things."

4 Waley's note: It means "Heaven deigned to help them; in its pity it protected them."

Chapter 68

1 Waley's note: Wang Bi says quite rightly that "士" is a "leader" of foot-soldiers. The leaders rode in war-chariots. However, Young and Ames' translation can be an alternative: "Those adept at being officers Do not display warlike emotions."

Chapter 69

1, 2 It is not "doubt," but "dare not."

3 These two lines can be translated as "This is what we call: To deploy troops as if without deploying, To strike out as if without an arm."

4 Waley's note: The Wang Bi commentary shows the order

in which these clauses should come.

5 Waley's note: i. e. pity.

Chapter 70

1 Waley's note: To have "neither ancestors nor lord" was to be a wild man, a savage. This is a metaphorical way of saying that all the sage did and said was related to a definite system of thought.

2 "则" here means "emulate." This sentence should be understood as "Even fewer emulate me."

3 It is "coarse-colth."

Chapter 71

1 For "病病", Chen Guying translates them as "who recognizes sickminded as sick-minded."

2 In Chen Guying text, these two sentences are moved to the end of the chapter based on the explanation by Jiang Xichang.

Chapter 72

1 Waley's note: Heaven.

2 Wang Bi comments on these two sentences: "When those in authority can not control the people, when the people can not put up with authority, then there will be a great disintegration in the relationship between the ruling and the ruled." So we might understand them as: "When the people no longer show fear for

the intimitation of the authority, then calamities are on the way."

3 Waley's note: Literally "that whereby they live," their livelihoods.

Chapter 73

1 Henricks translated these three sentences as "If you're brave in being daring, you'll be killed, If you're brave in not being daring, you'll live. With these two things, in one case there's profit, in the other there's harm."

2 This line belongs to Chapter 63, according to Ma Xunlun and Gao Heng.

Chapter 74

1 Wang Bi says, "奇" means "to put in a turmoil with intrigues," so it can be translated as "those who commit felonies."

2 Waley's note: Heaven, or its agents (pestilence, famine, lightning, earthquake, etc.).

3 Waley's note: Adaptation of a proverb meaning "let every man stick to his task."

Chapter 76

1 Chen Guying explains that "万物" is redundant, for in many texts, there are no such two characters.

2 It is often understood as "the mighty and formidable army

will be defeated."

Chapter 77

1 Here we take for reference the translation by Young and Ames: "Is not the Tao of Heaven like the drawing of a bow? If the aim is high then we lower our sights; If the aim is low then we raise them."

2 The sentences in parentheses are considered irrelevant to the text above in meaning.

Chapter 78

1 D. C. Lau translates this sentence as "This is because there is nothing that can take its place."

2 Waley's note: Seem, as we should say, to be paradoxes.

Chapter 79

1 According to Ma Xulun, "To requite injuries with good deeds" should be put before the sentence "安可以为善" in this chapter. I have to put the sentence at the beginning for Waley translated the three sentences into one in English.

2 D. C. Lau understands this sentence as "Therefore the sage takes the left-hand tally (The left-hand tally is the half held by the creditor), but extracts no payment from the people."

Chapter 80

1 The explanations given by Yan Lingfeng and Zhang Songru are "tens of and hundreds of contrivances".

2 "重" should be "important" instead of "again" or "twice". It means that "to make people regard that to die (in their native place) is important".

3 Waley explains, "The passage in inverted commas occurs (with trifling differences) in Zhuangzi (Ch. 10) as a description of life under the rule of the legendary agricultural Sage Shennong. The whole chapter can be understood in the past, present or future tense, as the reader desires."

Chapter 81

1 This should be "to benefit without injuring". Waley's note: To achieve the end without using the material means.

2 Chen Guying deletes the word "圣" based on the Silk Text B.

参考书目 Bibliography

1. 陈鼓应《老子注译及评介》,中华书局,1984 年。

2. 陈鼓应《老庄新论》,上海古籍出版社,1992 年。

3. 张松如《老子校读》,吉林人民出版社,1981 年。

4. 卢育三《老子释义》,天津古籍出版社,1987 年。

5. 张玉春、金国泰《老子注译》,巴蜀书社,1991 年。

6. 黄钊主编《道家思想史纳》,湖南师范大学出版社,1991 年。

7. 任继愈主编《中国道教史》,上海人民出版社,1990 年。

8. 张舜徽《周秦道论发微》,中华书局,1982 年。

9. 张立文主编《道》,中国人民大学出版社,1989 年。

10. 詹剑峰《老子其人其书及其道论》,湖北人民出版社,1982 年。

11. 亚瑟·韦利译著《道和德〈道德经〉及其在中国思想中的地位研究》,乔治·艾伦和安温有限公司,1934 年。

12. 刘殿爵译《老子道德经》,企鹅丛书,1963 年。

13. 杨有维、罗杰·艾米斯译《老子注译及其评介》,台湾中国资料中心,1981 年。

14. 林振述译《老子道德经和王弼注英译》,密执安中国研究文献,1977 年。

15. 初大告译《道德经》,海泽尔·沃森和维尼有限公司,1959 年。

16. 赫里蒙·毛利尔译《道之道》,剑桥大学出版社,

1982 年。

17. 韩禄伯译《老子德道经马王堆帛书新译》,麦克米兰公司,1989 年。

18. 刘殿爵《道德经马王堆帛书英译》,大卫·坎贝尔出版有限公司,1994 年。

1. Chen Guying, *Annotations on Laozi with Contemporary Chinese Translation*, China Book Company, 1984.

2. Chen Guying, *A New Commentary on Laozi and Zhuangzi*, Shanghai Classics Press, 1992.

3. Zhang Songru, *A Collation of Laozi with Textual Study*, Jilin People's Press, 1981.

4. Lu Yusan, *Exposition on Laozi*, Tianjin Classics Press, 1987.

5. ZhangYuchun and Jin Guotai, *Annotation and Modern Chinese Translation of Laozi*, Bashu Press, 1991.

6. Huang Zhao, ed. *An Outline of Taoist Thought*, Hunan Normal University Press, 1991.

7. Ren Jiyu, ed. *A History of Chinese Taoist Religion*, Shanghai People's Press, 1990.

8. Zhang Shunhui, *Exposition on the Subtle Meanings of Taoism in the Zhou and Qin Dynasties*, China Book Company, 1982.

9. Zhang Liwen, ed. *Dao*, Chinese People's University Press, 1989.

10. Zhan Jianfeng, *Laozi, His Book and His Taoism*, Hubei People's Press, 1982.

11. Arthur Waley, *The Way and Its Power, A Study of the Tao Te Ching and Its Place in Chinese Thought*, George Allen and Unwin Lit., London, 1934.

12. D. C. Lau, *Lao Tzu Tao Te Ching*, Penguin Books, 1963.

13. Rhett Y. W. Young and Roger T. Ames, *Laozi*, *Text*, *Notes and Coments*, Chinese Material Center, Taiwan, 1981.

14. Paul J. Lin, *A Translation of Lao Tzu's Tao Te Ching and Wang Bi's Commentary*, Michigan Papers in Chinese Studies, 1977.

15. Chu Takao, *Tao Te Ching*, Hazel Watson and Viney Ltd. , 1959.

16. Herrymon Maurer, *TAO*: *The Way of the Ways*, Cambridge University Press, 1982.

17. Robert Henricks, *Lao Tzu Te-Tao Ching*, *A New Translation Basea on the Recently Discovered Ma-wang-tui Texts*, Macmillan Publishing Company, 1989.

18. D. C. Lau, *Tao Te Ching Translation of the Ma Wang Tui Manuscripts*, David Campbell Publishers Ltd. , 1994.

图书在版编目(CIP)数据

老子:汉英对照/杨牧之主编．—海口:
南海出版公司,2013.4
(中华古典文化精粹)
ISBN 978-7-5442-6552-2

Ⅰ.①老… Ⅱ.①杨… Ⅲ.①道家-汉、英 Ⅳ.
①B223.11

中国版本图书馆 CIP 数据核字(2013)第 061460 号

ZHONGHUA GUDIAN WENHUA JINGCUI:LAOZI
中华古典文化精粹:老子

主　　编　杨牧之
副 主 编　霍宝珍
责任编辑　张　媛　李凤君
装帧设计　柏拉图创意机构
出版发行　南海出版公司　电话:(0898)66568508(出版)
65350227(发行)
地　　址　海南省海口市海秀中路 51 号星华大厦五楼
邮编:570206
电子信箱　nanhaicbgs@yahoo.com.cn
经　　销　新华书店
印　　刷　三河市三佳印刷装订有限公司
开　　本　890 毫米×1280 毫米　1/32
印　　张　11.25
字　　数　250 千
版　　次　2013 年 5 月第 1 版　2013 年 5 月第 1 次印刷
书　　号　ISBN 978-7-5442-6552-2
定　　价　23.00 元

First Edition 2013

ISBN 978 - 7 - 5442 - 6552 - 2

Published by
Nanhai Publishing Company
5th Floor, Xinghua Building, No. 51, Haixiu Middle Road, Haikou 570206, Hainan, China

Printed by
Sanheshi Sanjia Printing Company, Hebei, China

Printed in the People's Republic of China